THE LITTLE BOOK OF
Olive Oil

D1324960

Nicolas de Barry

Translated by
Louise Guiney

Flammarion

The Story of Olive Oil 6

Alphabetical Guide 22

Appendices

Alphabetical Guide

The alphabetical entries have been classified according to the following categories. Each category is indicated with a small colored square.

■ Olives Around the World

■ How Olive Oil is Cultivated and Produced

■ How Olive Oil is Used

The information given in each entry, together with cross-references indicated by asterisks, enables the reader to explore the world of olive oil.

THE STORY OF OLIVE OIL

With its gnarled trunks rising from the hillsides of Provence, Tuscany, and Greece*, the olive tree* looks as old as the world. It figures prominently in the history of the Mediterranean region, its chosen home. It has inspired legends, and occupies a central place in all the religions associated with this part of the globe: the olive was sacred to Isis and Athena, Moses, Christ, and Mohammed. No plant, with the possible exception of the grapevine, has enjoyed the same degree of mythic fame and mystical resonance. In our own time, recent research has brought olive oil back into fashion, giving it a primary role in the cuisine of the new millennium. Studies conducted on the island of Crete, where olive oil and wine are staples of the daily diet, show that the local population are particularly well protected against cardio-vascular disease, certain types of cancer, and the effects of aging.

A Millenarian Native of the Mediterranean

The olive tree first appeared in Asia Minor, during the twelfth millennium before our era. There were in fact vast forests of olive trees which remained uncultivated by humans for six millennia. It then spread from Syria, through Anatolia to Greece, and on to Egypt and Crete. In 1600 B.C. the Phoenicians began planting olive trees throughout Greece and around the entire Mediterranean Basin. In 600 B.C. olive trees were brought to Gaul through the port that is now Marseilles. They played a major economic role under the Romans, who planted groves throughout their empire and installed presses (see Pressing) that were ultra-modern for the period. The cultivation of olives declined following the barbarian and early Arabian invasions, but was revived at the time of the Crusades, due to the rise of Venice* as a commercial power. Spanish and Portuguese conquistadors carried olive trees across the Atlantic, planting them mainly in Argentina, Mexico, and California. Most recently, olive trees have been successfully introduced in South Africa and Australia.

Archeological remains provide proof that the olive tree dates back to the very distant past, as does human recognition of olive oil's beneficial properties. Surviving artifacts indicate that olive oil was manufactured as early as the Neolithic and Chalcolithic periods. Over one hundred olive presses dating from the Iron Age were found in the Philistine city of Ekron. On the basis of this discovery, archeologists have calculated that city's annual production of olive oil at about 125,000 gallons.

Olive trees were extensively cultivated by the Minoan peoples (2700–1200 B.C.) living on the island of Crete. A bas-relief at the

Small phials for tasting olive oil.

THE STORY OF OLIVE OIL

Jars (sixteenth century B.C.) found on the Minoan site of Akrotiri, Isle of Santorin.

entrance to the Palace of Knossos shows a sacred bull leaping towards an olive tree, while a carving on a stone sarcophagus shows an olive tree standing behind the sacrificial altar. Decorative motifs featuring stylized olive leaves and blossoms have also been found on numerous amphorae. This is the earliest evidence of a product "branded" for export: most of the olive oil consumed in Egypt was shipped from Minoan Crete.

In the kingdom of the Pharaohs, olive oil was used not only as a foodstuff, but also as perfume and for embalming the dead. Mummies of the twentieth dynasty (1200–1090 B.C.) were decorated with braided olive branches. But it is in ancient Greece that the olive tree—the creation, according to mythology*, of the goddess Athena—made its greatest cultural impact. It appears frequently in art* of the period, being depicted in paintings and sculptures and effigies of the maternal goddess were often carved from olive wood. Olive trees also appear frequently in literature*, notably in works by Aeschylus and Homer. Olive oil was used in medicine, and Galen codified its medicinal applications. It was also useful for making perfumes (olive oil was used as a fixative in which plants were steeped to extract their fragrances), for massages and cleansing, as well as in the preparations for athletic events. Kings and priests were anointed with olive oil and royal scepters were made from olive wood. The descendents of the gods were often born in the shade of an olive tree . . .

Touring Olive Country

From ancient Greece, through the golden ages of the Ottoman, Venetian, and Portuguese empires, to the modern era, its propagation has been encouraged and olive oil has been a part of the daily diet for most Mediterranean peoples. The Greeks are the largest consumers, at five gallons annually per capita, about the same amount as their ancestors consumed over two thousand years ago.

Regions renowned for their olive groves are among those most popular with tourists. Catalonia and Andalusia in Spain*; Tuscany, Liguria, Umbria, Sicily, and Sardinia in Italy*; the Peloponnese peninsula and the Greek islands; the coast of Turkey*; Tunisia; and Provence in France*, not to mention California. This fascination for the Mediterranean countryside has thus contributed to the fame of olive oil.

Spain, the leading producer of olive oil worldwide, has over five million acres planted in olive trees. The best oils come from Catalonia and Andalusia. The hot Andalusian summers and natural irrigation* provided by the melting snows of the Sierra Nevada are ideal for the evenly spaced rows of olive and orange trees, seen everywhere in this region—as are bulls, of course. After a bullfight at the Feria de Sevilla, what could be better than dining on the delectable local dishes inevitably prepared with olive oil? Strict quality standards have been established for the AOC (Origin Officially Guaranteed)

The Olive Press. Miniature from Pliny's *Natural History*, sixteenth century manuscript. Biblioteca Marciana, Venice.

oils of Baena, Priego de Cordoba, Sierra Magina, and Sierra Segura, all located in the Cordova and Jaén regions. Moving northward between Tarragona and Lleida in Catalonia, other high quality oils, such as Garrigues and Siurana, are ideal when combined with a paella or snails Catalán.

In Portugal*, groves of centuries-old olive trees stretch from the Douro to the Algarve, as far as the eye can see. Cultivation* of olives, which was in sharp decline, is now expanding once more. The landscape has been transfigured and the native oil is naturally organic. Visitors to Lisbon's old town should stop at a good bistro—where Fernando Pessoa drowned his dreams of distant Brazil in cup after cup of coffee—and order the local dish known as *bacalhau*, cod cooked with potatoes, peppers, tomatoes, and olives, all liberally sprinkled with a thick, fruity olive oil.

In Italy, different regions produce different types of oil, each with its own distinctive properties. Olive oil is fruitier in the south, in the heel of the Italian boot and in Sicily; it is milder in Venezia and Liguria, yet perfectly balanced in Tuscany and Latium. It is omnipresent in Italian cuisine—*carpaccio* with olive oil, *pasta alio-olio*, buffalo mozzarella sprinkled with Campania oil, Neapolitan pizza—the list is endless. Combined with a dash of Sicilian lemon juice or balsamic vinegar, olive oil is also a standard ingredient in dressings for salads and vegetables cooked *al dente*. Italian olive oils bear noble names: the great aristocratic families of Tuscany and Sicily produce their own oils, just as French châteaux produce their own wines. A tour of the Tuscan villas famed for producing the world's best olive oils is a spell-binding experience, one that reflects the inherent magic of the oils themselves and makes it easier to accept the price, which can be extremely high.

In Italy olive oil may be an aristocrat, but it is a commoner in Greece* and Turkey*. These rival siblings today share the ancient olive groves first planted by Alexander the Great, the man whose conquests extended as far as India—where he introduced the toga, now called the sari—and olive oil, still used today as an ointment for ayurvedic massage*. The best Greek oils come from the Peloponnese peninsula and Crete, where they are produced in large quantities by cooperatives* which often produce a high quality result. Olive oil costs next to nothing here, and is sometimes imbibed by the glass. In Turkey, small independent olive growers take their harvest to state cooperatives, which extract the oil and market it throughout the country. A specialty of Turkey, Greece, and neighboring countries is

A bottle of finest French oil.

Terraced olive grove in Provence.

the traditional *mezes*, a range of appetizers so varied that no single list could include them all, but they all have one thing in common: they are made with olive oil.

In the dry climate* of the Middle East* and North Africa*, olive groves, sometimes planted on the edge of the desert, are living records of local history. In Palestine and Lebanon, they are scarred by warfare; in Libya, they are austere and geometrical; lush and green in Tunisia, the second-ranked producer worldwide, flooding our tables with its fruity, unpretentious oils. An hour or two spent on the terrace of a modest hostelry in some little Tunisian port, enjoying a meal of mussels or plain grilled fish cooked with freshly pressed olive oil, is a good incentive for abandoning the life of luxury. Here, simple uncomplicated pleasures are a true treat for the palate.

How Is Olive Oil Made?

Olive oil, like all good things, is made according to methods that are both simple and complex. Simple, because all you have to do is harvest the fruits from a tree that produces generous amounts, press them to extract their "juice," then decant the juice to separate the pure oil from the water—an easy task, since oil is lighter than water and rises to the surface naturally. In the past, pressing was done with the feet or by placing the crushed olives in a cloth

Monessargues mill in southern France.

and squeezing. Does this mean that anyone with a few olive trees in the garden can make their own oil?

Olive harvest, Piene-Haut, France.

Not really. Oleiculture is actually difficult and meticulous work. First, the trees must be planted in favorable ground (and, in particular, protected from freezes*); the selected varieties* must be well adapted to the local soil and climate; and the trees must be irrigated.

Once planted, they must be regularly pruned*, treated for parasites* (notably the olive fly), etc. Choosing the best time and method for harvesting is essential: whether the olives should be allowed to fall from the tree by themselves, at the risk of damaging much of the crop, or picked early; whether they should be picked by hand, using a stick or knife, or by the modern vibration method. The quality of the harvested olives will depend in part on the method chosen. Most importantly, all traces of rot and debris must be carefully removed. Although often invisible to the naked eye, this can affect the oleic acid content, and thus the quality and classification*, of the oil.

Olive mills* must produce an "extra virgin" oil with a shelf life of at least two years, i.e. the minimum level of quality demanded by consumers. Unlike wine, olive oil does not improve with age. Compared with refining*, pressing* produces a more wholesome product, rich in vitamins A and E and in monounsaturated fatty acids, that is beneficial to the health*. However, pressed oil is also particularly vulnerable to the development of bacteria and mildews, that can diminish quality. The shelf life of olive oil is thus significantly affected by bottling and storage*, and its packaging should protect the oil from air, light, and heat. Gourmet chefs will then combine the oil with other delicious ingredients, preferably leaving it unheated to preserve its beneficial properties.

For consumers, the next problem is choice. There is no official olive oil guide or listing to use as a reference, and ordering by mail can be risky in view of factors described above. However, as for wine, there are some basic rules to follow. First, it is advisable to taste the oil before purchasing it. If this is not possible, careful examination of the label is important. It should include the term "extra virgin." The phrase "first cold pressing" is redundant, since all "extra virgin" oils are cold pressed. The region of origin can also be meaningless, except for AOC (Origin Officially Guaranteed) labels. The names to look out for are, in Spain, Baena, Les Garrigues, Priego de Cordoba, Sierra Magina, Sierra Segura, Siurana, and in France, Les Baux and Nyons. These labels are governed by strict production standards and subjected to frequent inspection. Lastly, the only obligatory date, that of the bottling, is not an indication of freshness, since the oil may have been pressed long before it was bottled. It is regrettable that the date of pressing, though the most important, is rarely specified. In short, the best guarantee of quality is the name of the producer, whether independent or cooperative, and then only after an initial tasting and evaluation of the "growth*."

Freshly pressed Andalusian oils.

The Many Uses for Olive Oil

For most of us ordinary mortals, olive oil is used only as a dressing for salads. Its other virtues are often unfamiliar. In fact, olive oil is not just used in cooking, but also in medicine and cosmetics *.

Olive oil's benefits to the health* were well known in ancient times: Hippocrates, Pliny, Galen, Dioscorides, and Averroes all used it as an ingredient for medications and, especially, as a basic ingredient for ointments*. When combined with essential oils extracted from other plants, it has a special place in traditional folk remedies, which inspire today's proponents of natural medicine. Its warming, soothing properties make it ideal as an ingredient in massage ointments. The ancients used it to oil their bodies prior to athletic events and restore muscles and limbs in an early form of physiotherapy. The olive leaf is also a natural fungicide.

Olive oil and olive leaves are also widely used as cosmetics. The leaf is rich in antioxidants and regenerates the cells of the epidermis. Olive oil protects the skin and adds luster to the hair. Alone or in

combination with substances from other plants (through macera-
tion), it was used daily by the Greeks and Romans before and after
bathing. At a much later date, it became the basic ingredient in soap.
In the 1950s, "Palmolive Green," made with palm and olive oils, was
the market leader in its sector, and it is still popular today.

Today, when the extensive mass production of cosmetics and foodstuffs raises the specter of cost-cutting practices that could be harmful
to our health, olive oil retains its image as a "healthy" household
product—to be found in the kitchen, bathroom, and medicine cabinet.

Furthermore, recent research into the effects of diet on cardio-
vascular diseases, cancer, and aging has shown that olive oil, contrary
to a belief common just twenty years ago, contains elements that are
useful for preventing these conditions. Olive oil's chemical structure
provides the basis for its biological and therapeutic virtues: it is composed of triglycerides, or monounsaturated fatty acids (mainly oleic
acid), whereas animal fats are made up of saturated fatty acids, and
soy and sunflower oils contain polyunsaturated fatty acids. This is

the distinction most closely associated with the production of "good" or "bad" cholesterol in the blood. Olive oil also contains tocopherols (primarily alpha-tocopherol) and carotene, which produce vitamins E and A respectively. When combined with polyphenols, these two vitamins act as powerful antioxidants. Unlike polyunsaturated oils, olive oil does not contribute to the retardation in cellular regeneration that is the principal cause of aging; its vitamin E content actually increases the organism's own self-protective capacity. Statistical studies based on population samples from various parts of the world have awarded the "best health" prize to Crete, where the traditional diet is rich in wine and olive oil. Olive oil is also recommended for the treatment of gastric acidity and ulcers. It prevents the formation of gall stones, improves the functioning of the gall bladder and, taken alone on an empty stomach, facilitates the digestive process.

But enough of science—let's talk about pleasure! "Mediterranean" cuisine is influenced by Italian, Greek, and even Middle Eastern dishes, including pasta, salads, vegetables cooked *al dente* (which preserves their vitamins), and, of course, olive oil. This sun-drenched cuisine has inspired restaurants all around the world. However, consumers in northern Europe and America remain relatively impervious to this revolution, continuing to use olive oil only sparingly. Thought to have a stronger taste and to be more expensive than other oils, it is used mainly preparing *hors d'œuvres* and salads. Few families in these countries cook with olive oil, preferring butter. And yet, wider use of olive oil is highly recommended: it enhances the taste of other ingredients, is ideal for dishes that are only briefly exposed to heat, and is more digestible than other oils or fats. Jacques Chibois, in his book entitled *Olive Oil*, even includes recipes for desserts and sherbets made with olive oil!

Small wonder that the ancients believed the olive tree, its fruit and its oil, were a gift from the gods. Such a useful tree could hardly have come about by chance... Today, beliefs have changed, but the olive is as much a treasure as ever. Enjoy your journey to the sunny lands of the olive!

Aioli

When we think of Mediterranean cuisine, garlic and olive oil immediately spring to mind. However, although garlic was relished by the Egyptians and the Romans, it was spurned by the ancient Greeks. In Spain*, under Alfonzo de Castilla (fourteenth century), the use of garlic by aristocrats was banned! Olive oil and garlic have not always been inseparable companions everywhere along the Mediterranean coast. The mayonnaise-type sauce known as *aioli*, an almost unalloyed blend of these two ingredients, is nonetheless virtually synonymous with the local cuisine. It is served as an accompaniment to bouillabaisse—as *rouille*, after the addition of pimentos and/or saffron—and other dishes, but is most often associated with the dish of poached cod and boiled vegetables that has assumed its name. To make *aioli* sauce: place 4 large cloves of garlic in a mortar and crush to a smooth paste with a pestle. Add 1 egg yolk, salt, and pepper. Continue to beat with the pestle, adding olive oil in a thin stream until the mayonnaise becomes stiff. An *aioli* sauce should be used immediately, as it will not keep until the next day.

Antiquity

The oldest olive oil jars (dating back to 6,000 B.C.) were discovered at Jericho, in Palestine. The earliest "cultural" traces of olive oil appear in Egypt, on bas-reliefs in the tombs of the pharaohs. Olive presses are depicted on the frescoes of a *mastaba* (funerary monument) at Sakkarah dating from the

fourth or fifth dynasty (2,500 B.C.). Curiously, although numerous vestiges show that olive oil was widely used by the Egyptians in cosmetics*, medicinal ointments, and as fuel for lighting and religious rituals, there is little evidence of its inclusion in their cuisine. It is possible that the Egyptians had little use for it: according to Theophrastus, Egyptian oil "has a strong odor," attributing this to the practice of late harvesting*, which increased yield at the expense of taste.

Archeological excavations at the Minoan palaces at Knossos and Phaistos in Crete—a paradise for olive trees*—uncovered huge amphorae

A bowl of *aioli* with its ingredients: fine olive oil and garlic.

Left: *The Olive Harvest*. Greek amphora, sixth century B.C. British Museum, London.

Following page: *The Olive Press*. Mosaic, Saint-Romain-en-Gal, third century A.D. Musée des Antiquités Nationales, Saint-Germain-en-Laye.

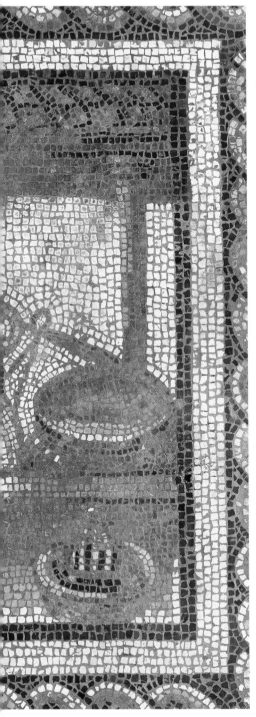

He stepped down into the vaulted treasure-chamber of his father, a spacious room, where gold and bronze lay piled, and raiment in coffers, and fragrant olive oil in plenty . . .

Homer, *The Odyssey*

(almost six feet in height) used for storing olive oil. The storerooms of the Knossos palace could thus hold as many as 250,000 gallons of olive oil! Crete exported its oil mainly to Middle and Late Empire Egypt. The cultivation* of this flourishing and lucrative crop ceased in 1450 B.C., when the island was ravaged by an earthquake.

In Greece*, the cultivation of olive groves became a foundation stone of Hellenistic civilization, and allusions to olive oil in Greek literature* are frequent. Olive oil was used by the Greeks in various domains: religion*, sports, and health*. The Greeks recognized the same three types of olive oil as we do today. Only virgin oils were used in the preparation of meals; the others were reserved for cosmetics and lighting. Virgin olive oil for the table, a primary source of nutritional lipids, was served cold at meals for seasoning cooked dishes, salads, raw vegetables, cheeses, etc. Oil from the second pressing* was used for cooking and frying. The people of modern Greece consume almost the same amount of oil per capita as in ancient times—five gallons per person per year—making this country the leading consumer of olive oil in the world.

Vincent van Gogh, *Olive Trees*, Saint-Rémy, 1889. Oil on canvas. Whitney Museum, of American Art, New York.

In ancient Rome, and throughout the land that is Italy* today, olive oil consumption was also high: the classical author Cato the Elder recommended a ration of two gallons per slave per month! However, the cultivation* of olive trees did not really become widespread until 200 B.C. Olive oil was eventually transported by Rome's merchant navy of galleys to the outermost limits of the vast empire, all the way to India.

■ Art

In 1957, in the Ahaggar mountains of Algeria, cave paintings dating from the fifth to the second millennium B.C. were discovered. Indisputably the oldest paintings of the olive tree*, they depicted men crowned with olive branches (see Symbolism). Olive trees are frequently shown—notably in harvesting* scenes—on Greek vases and amphorae used for holding oil in antiquity*. The Madrid Museum of Archeology displays a bell-shaped bowl, dated 340 B.C., illustrating

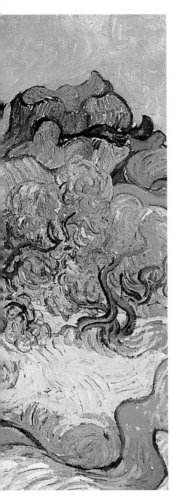

against the yellow earth, rosy-violet or orange-like, almost reddish-ocher. But it's very hard, very hard. But it suits me and encourages me to work in gold and silver. And one day I'll achieve my own personal impression, as with sunflowers for the yellows."

■ California

The growth in demand for olive oil in the United States in recent years has been phenomenal: consumption increases by twenty percent every year, and there is no sign of the trend slowing in the near future. As elsewhere, the reason for this is olive oil's beneficial reputation in terms of health, as part of the famous Mediterranean diet. Although home production is a mere one percent of the annual world output, far behind market leaders such as Spain, the 1998 production total was still a respectable 325,000 gallons, or seven hundred tons. The olive crop was worth over sixty-six million dollars. ninety-nine percent of American olive oil is grown in California, partly because the climate of this region is especially favorable, and partly because people in this part of the world are particularly health-conscious. Many of the 1,200 farms are organic, reflecting such concerns. However, only five of these growers cultivate an area larger than five hundred acres, and two-thirds farm no more than twenty acres. The total area farmed in 1997 was 35,300 acres, tiny in comparison to other countries. Many olive growers in this part of the world do not rely on olives as the only source of their income, offering farm experience holidays and retreats, as well as olive-based products such as soaps.

Athena's victory over Poseidon in their competition to become the patron god of Attica, thanks to the olive tree (see Mythology). Innumerable Renaissance paintings of *Christ on the Mount of Olives** gave the olive tree a supporting role in the overall composition. More recently however, this tree assumed a new dimension in paintings by Vincent van Gogh and Paul Cézanne. As van Gogh wrote, "Olive trees are very distinctive and I am struggling to grasp that. They're silvery, sometimes bluish, sometimes bronze-green, white

27

■ CLASSIFICATION
Cold Pressed and Virgin

The rules governing the classification of olive oil worldwide were established by the member nations of the International Olive Oil Council. Supplemented by the codex standard formulated by the joint commission of the FAO and the WHO (the United Nations' specialized agencies for agriculture and health, respectively), they have established the following classifications:

• Virgin olive oil: obtained exclusively from cold pressing*.

• Extra virgin olive oil: also obtained exclusively from cold pressing, with a maximum acidity content of one percent (a sign of quality and purity).

• Fine virgin olive oil: maximum acidity content two percent.

• Standard virgin olive oil: maximum acidity content 3.3 percent.

• Virgin lighting oil: unfit for human consumption, may be refined*.

• Refined olive oil: in common with other vegetable oils, refined olive oil is high in lipid content, but its distinctive fragrance and flavor are diminished.

• Olive oil: a blend of virgin and refined oils.

• Olive cake oil: oil refined from olive cakes made of the residue from pressing.

In practice, almost all olive oils sold on the retail market, even the least costly, are classified "extra virgin." This classification is therefore far from adequate for evaluating the quality of the product or for informing consumers. It establishes a "guaranteed minimum" of purity, but does not specify whether or not the oil is fresh, where it comes from, whether it is a blend made from two different harvests, and so on. Consumers should look for the name of the growth*, the name of the grower (if specified), the brand, the distributor, or (better yet) buy direct from the mill* whenever possible.

Extra virgin olive oils from Latium, Provence, Sicily, Istria, and Sardinia.

■ Climate

The olive tree*, a native of the Mediterranean coast, is rarely found at high altitudes. In order for its fruit to ripen properly, it needs mild winters—as temperatures lower than 15°F or minus 7°C (see Freeze) are fatal—sufficient rain in autumn and spring, and hot dry summers. Mean annual temperatures should range from 60°F to 72°F (16°C to 22°C) and annual rainfall, supplemented if necessary by modern irrigation* systems, must be at least 8.5 inches (220 mm).

Following a period of winter dormancy lasting from November to February, the olive's growing cycle begins in March-April, with the appearance of the new shoots and the buds

which will produce flowers and fruit. Olive trees blossom in May-June. The fruit develops over the summer and ripens in October. Depending on the variety*, harvesting takes place from September (for green olives) until February (for late-ripening varieties*). In countries with hotter climates, such as Tunisia (see North Africa), this cycle begins and ends earlier. Attempts have been made to acclimatize the olive tree to northern regions with mild climates: in northern Italy*, for example. Olive groves were once common on the banks of Lake Lugano in Switzerland, and they have recently been re-introduced there by Claudio Tamborini.

Returning home from market, Morocco. Photograph by J. Marando.

■ Consecrated Oil

Olive oil is considered a gift of God in the many regions* where it is used for religious sacraments. "Consecrated oil" is in fact olive oil. In the Book of Exodus (30: 22-31), "...the Lord spake unto Moses, saying, Take thou also unto thee principal spices, of pure myrrh five hundred shekels, and of sweet cinnamon half so much, even two hundred and fifty shekels, and of sweet calamus two hundred and fifty shekels, and of cassia five hundred shekels, after the shekel of the sanctuary, and of olive oil a hin: and thou shalt make it an oil of holy ointment, an ointment compound after the art of the apothecary: it shall be an holy anointing oil. And thou shalt anoint the tabernacle of the congregation . . . and the altar of the incense, and the altar of burnt offering ... and thou shalt sanctify them, that they may be most holy: whatsoever toucheth them shall be holy. And thou shalt anoint Aaron and his sons, and consecrate them, that they may minister unto me in the priest's office. And thou shalt speak unto the children of Israel, saying, This shall be an holy anointing oil unto me throughout your generations."

The baptism of King Clovis (466–511) by Saint Remy was archetypical of consecration for Christian kings as the way in which divine intervention was made visible: through the miracle of a sacred phial carried by the Holy Ghost, in the guise of a dove, and containing the consecrated oil for anointing the king of the Franks. A phial of consecrated oil, believed never to be emptied of its precious contents,

was preserved for a long time in the abbey of Saint Remy (no longer standing today) in Rheims, east of Paris.

In Christian liturgy, the consecration of oils during the mass celebrated on Maundy Thursday is accompanied with these words: "We pray thee,

Lord, to bless this oil that thou hast caused to be made by the olive tree*, that immortal tree, so that it may serve to heal the body and the soul." Christians of the Orthodox Churches attribute numerous cures to holy oils, which sometimes flow miraculously.

On 17 January 1983, in the Orthodox church of Our Lady of Sufanieh in Syria (see Middle East), it was reported that consecrated oil flowed from the holy icon and also from the floor of a neighboring terrace on which the Virgin was said to have appeared.

The Baptism of Clovis. Miniature from *Les Grandes Chroniques de France*, 1380. Bibliothèque Municipale, Castres.

Cooperatives

At various times in history, those depending on agriculture for their livelihood have formed cooperative organizations in order to relieve the problems associated with natural or economic difficulties. Cooperatives are most common in the wine and olive oil industries. Just as wine growers joined forces in response to the late nineteenth-century phylloxera epidemic, olive oil producers also recognized the

need to unite following the catastrophic freeze* of 1929. Olives were often not the principal crop for these growers, and as a result the development of cooperatives was essential as an economic strategy for strengthening the sector. The cooperative movement proved its effectiveness during the catastrophic freeze of 1956. Although not all of the cooperatives survived, many did manage to recover from the disaster.

In Italy*, small family groves are the rule, though there are a few cooperatives, whereas in Spain* and Greece* they are omnipresent. In Turkey*, where cooperatives were introduced by government decree, some have as many as 30,000 members.

However, as in the wine industry, the disadvantage of the cooperative system lies in its tendency to blend products from different origins and of different grades (sometimes of mediocre value), which can impair overall quality. Due to the relatively small supply and the substantial quantities of olives harvested from ill-tended ornamental groves (an acre or so planted around a holiday villa, for example), many cooperatives are reduced to pressing large quantities of poor quality olives.

However, the best cooperatives recognize the value of careful selection: they sort the olives according to origin and grade, and process them in separate lots.

Now at the harbour's head is a long-leaved olive tree, and hard by is a pleasant cave and shadowy, sacred to the nymphs . . .

Homer, *The Odyssey*

Virgin olive oil from the Jean-Marie Cornille mill, Vallée des Baux Oil Cooperative.

Théodore
Chassériau, *Esther
At Her Toilet*,
1841.
Oil on canvas.
Musée du Louvre,
Paris.

■ Cosmetics

Many olive lovers are familiar with the famous *Savon de Marseille*, an olive oil based soap*, and also with the "Palmolive Green" soap popular in the 1950s. Due to cost and changes in fashion, olive oil has gradually disappeared from cosmetic formulas, but its newly discovered properties now herald its return to favor.

In antiquity* olive oil was the base for all cosmetics. The Egyptians used it for the heat extraction and collection of fragrant essences. These oils, scented with jasmine, rose, herbs, myrrh, etc., were used to massage the body following a bath, often cold, so that the skin would be firm and well scented. Phials of fragrant oils* were offered as gifts to house guests. Finally, olive oil was used for embalming the dead.

The Greeks also used olive oil for after-bath massages. In *The Characters*, Theophrastus satirizes misers who come to the baths with a small phial or with rancid oil. The phial of olive oil was the symbol* of civilisation: when Ulysses reached the Isle of the Phaeacians after being shipwrecked, he was presented by Nausicaa with a suit of new clothing and a phial of oil. He acknowledged the gift thus: "I shall wash away the sea foam on my shoulders, and anoint myself with this oil, that has for so long been a stranger to my skin." At the gymnasium, the Greeks used olive oil for relaxing the muscles, especially before hand-to-hand combat.

Ephebes Bathing.
Antique bowl
with red figures
attributed to
Euphronios,
c. 510 B.C.
Antikenmuseum,
Berlin.

In the Middle East*, olive oil is still the most common body care cosmetic. A few drops of rose-scented olive oil are used to anoint the heads of loved ones and for religious rites (see Religion). Lastly, thousands of miles from its native Mediterranean Basin, olive oil is used in traditional Indian medicine for massage*. Olive leaves also have beneficial properties, and they have been a feature of the pharmacopoeia since antiquity*. As with olive oil, they are enjoying a new popularity in health* care today. Extremely rich in fatty acid, olive leaves have antioxidant properties that protect the epidermis against free radicals, the major cause of ageing in the skin. They also stimulate the natural immune reaction that accelerates cellular regeneration, and act as a fungicide and detoxifier. Highly recommended for healthful living: a regime combining olive oil massages and the "Cretan" diet.

◼ Cost

Consumers are often perplexed by the wide variations in the cost for olive oil. Even when relatively inexpensive, it is still considerably more costly than other oils (sunflower, corn, peanut, and so on). Why? Because every step in the production process is costly. The olive tree* grows slowly and requires constant attention (pruning*, irrigation*). Harvesting, still largely manual, is labor-intensive. Extraction by pressing* is more costly than distillation. And, lastly, olive oil is more perishable than other oils, and thus requires especially careful packaging*. However, setting aside the difference in cost, the choice of oil is primarily a matter of personal taste and a desire for quality. Because of its strong taste, olive oil is used by many mainly in salads. The Italians and the Greeks, on the other hand, use olive oil for cooking as well as for seasoning, and it is an ingredient in almost all the dishes typical of these countries. It pays to remember, however, that if the aroma of a more expensive oil subtly enhances uncooked dishes, the ordinary grades are amply sufficient for cooking and frying.

Cost also varies substantially from one olive oil to another. Taster* Eric Verdier has therefore ranked olive oils in five categories, at retail costs ranging from $4 a quart to $26 a pint! This discrepancy can be daunting to the novice consumer who, in response to advertising, may be willing to pay more for an oil from Tuscany or the Baux Valley, neglecting varieties that are less well known but just as good. Actually, in view of the huge diversity among existing products, the best selection criteria are still personal taste and value for money.

Lastly, well-known brands or own-label olive oils sold by supermarket chains do offer quality oils at competitive prices, although they cannot claim to equal the greatest growths*. This is possible because of the high volumes involved, and a policy of selecting and blending oils from various sources, especially Spain* and Tunisia (see North Africa), major producers of standard quality oils.

Cylindrical olive crusher, second or third century A.D., found on the Roman site of Volubilis, Morocco.

Crushing

Crushing the olives prior to pressing* is the first step in the process of producing olive oil. After harvesting*, the olives are transported to the mill*, where the miller will decide how long they should be stored—usually a few days, according to their ripeness—before being crushed. He also decides whether they need to be sorted, and, if necessary, when to cleanse them to remove all traces of chemical sprays, etc. The crushing can then begin. The principle is simple: the olives are crushed—with or without their pits, depending on local custom—until they are reduced to a paste which can then be beaten to facilitate pressing. In the past, and at a few elite mills still today, the crushed olives were then allowed to drain. This step produces a pure unpressed oil marketed under the name *fleur d'olive*, or premium virgin oil.

Crushing is just as important as pressing, and it is carried out with particular care. The oldest known circular millstone for crushing olives was discovered in the city of Olynthus (Asia Minor), which was destroyed in 348 B.C. by Philip of Macedonia. This millstone is clearly designed for crushing olives rather than milling flour, thus proving the antiquity of the olive oil making process.

Cylindrical stone rollers, some of them ridged, have been found in Syria and North Africa. The Romans used cylindrical grindstones of the *mola* type, which are rolled perpendicularly, and also the *trapetum*—described by Cato in the second century B.C.—several examples of which were found at Pompeii. The *trapetum* crushes the olives against the sides of the mortar, rather than against its base. Although this device is more effective, it is hard to build, due to the difficulty of calculating the exact distance between millstone and mortar. As a result, the *mola* came back into fashion at the

end of the Roman era. Perpendicular millstones using animal power (mule, horse, ox, or camel, depending on the country) to turn the roller appeared during the Middle Ages, and are still in use today. This technique is slow but steady, and crushes the fruit completely, pit and all.

In the eighteenth century, animals were gradually replaced by water power, and the single grindstone by two or three grindstones installed one above the other. The most recent development, of course, is electricity. But the old techniques—and sometimes even manual crushing—continue to be used here and there. Certain archaic techniques are sometimes more profitable for small volumes of production.

Alziari mill, Nice.

■ Cultivation

The olive tree* is easy to propagate. Cuttings taken from a mature tree will produce sprouts, after replanting. Trees can also be grown from olive pits, but it takes at least four years before the sprout will grow large enough to be transplanted. Growing new trees from cuttings is the most frequently used method. As early as the first century A.D., Columella advised as follows: "From the tree, cut straight and vigorous young branches of a size the hand can grasp, i.e. the diameter of a tool handle." New cuttings are rooted in nurseries, and transplanted later. The roots of an olive tree can also be pulled up and divided. When transplanted, these rootlets will put out new branches.

Today, specialists propagate olive trees in nurseries using one of two methods: planting olive pits, or rooting semi-woody cuttings. Pits will produce irregularly shaped but extremely hardy trees which are used solely as supports for grafts. Semi-woody cuttings produce a selection of more evenly shaped trees, from which branches are then cut for replanting. Young branches, about one year old, can be taken from these trees and cultivated in greenhouses; this is a more costly procedure, but the trees will develop rapidly and can be transplanted within two

years. Once they have been planted in a grove, the trees can be grafted with one of the varieties* selected, or the young branches are grafted onto older trees in order to give them a "spurt of youth."

Today grafts are inserted under the bark of the support tree using one of three methods: "quill" (for younger trees), "crown" (for older trees), or "plate." In the *Georgics*, Virgil describes two ancient methods—shield grafting and slit grafting—and their beneficial effect on the olive tree: "In a short time a large tree with fertile branches rises towards the sky, wondering at the sight of these new leaves and fruits which are not its own."

Alexandre Dumas.

■ **Dumas (Alexandre)** Famed historical novelist Alexandre Dumas (1802–1870) was also renowned for his appreciation of gastronomy*. Dumas believed that olive oil was the only acceptable oil, and remarked in passing that it was also the most commonly used, and least likely to turn rancid.

This somewhat surprising encomium is perhaps not devoid of chauvinism, for he also says: "Although Italy* and Spain* are blanketed in olive trees*, it is from these two countries that the worst oils come: producers, in order to double their yield, allow the olives to turn rancid. This advanced state of decomposition endows the oil pressed from them with an unbearable reek of decay. The same is true of the oils from Greece*, Syria, and Egypt … In my view, the freshest, clearest, and longest lasting is *lucques* oil, followed by virgin oil, green oil, and the fine oil of Aix, Grasse, and Nice." Dumas's opinion is no longer valid today, due to modern developments in the cultivation* of the olive tree, and recent developments which have led to the emergence of the Côte d'Azur as a prime producing region (see Regions).

41

■ FLAVORINGS AND FRAGRANCES
Herbs and Spices

Before the invention of the distillation process, the main method for extracting fragrance essences was by *enfleurage*. Blossoms, herbs, or woods were macerated in hot or cold baths of animal fat or vegetable oil. This operation was repeated several times, until the medium was completely saturated with the fragrance essence. In antiquity*, the medium used for the extraction bath was often olive oil. In the eighteenth century, heat *enfleurage* was still practiced, particularly for extracting essence of rose. At the end of the process, the oil retained the fragrance—the level of concentration could be varied—and could be used as a scent (or for the bath, the house, and garments) and, because of the inherent properties possessed by both oil and plants, in cosmetics*.

Facing page: Olive oil flavored with pimento.

"Frantoia" flavored oils (pimento, garlic, sage, oregano, and rosemary) from Barbera, Palermo.

Today there is renewed interest in scented oils for cosmetic use, particularly in countries with warm climates. In India, women maintain the beauty of their hair with ointments made of oil: olive oil for the wealthy, copra oil for those of more modest means. In Brazil, body oil for application during or after the daily shower is the most widely used beauty care product. Although olive oil is no longer an ingredient in mass market cosmetics, it is relatively easy to make scented olive oil at home simply by macerating herbs or spices (anise, bay leaf, citrus peel and so on) in the oil.

For cooking, modern trends have encouraged a vogue for olive oils flavored with white truffle, basil, pimento, mixed herbs, garlic—the list is endless. The principle here is the same as that used in perfumery: the oil acquires the fragrance and flavor of the substances macerated in it. The latter are then often left in the bottle, more for their aesthetic appeal than for their gastronomic value. The Italian olive oil producer Ursini, at the San Giovanni abbey in Venere, also offers oils pressed from a mixture of olives and citrus peel (orange, lemon, tangerine).

It is easy to flavor olive oil at home and has the additional advantage of ensuring that no artificial flavorings or preservatives will be used. But home-flavored oil must be used quickly, since it may turn rancid sooner than pure olive oil.

■ FRANCE

Olive groves in France cover an area of only about 50,000 acres, or one percent of the area devoted to them in Spain*. In recent years, olive oil production in France has fallen to ten percent of the levels recorded less than a century ago. The 1956 freeze that ravaged the olive groves of Provence is often blamed for this decline, but other factors accelerated the process: the transfer of olive growing to Tunisia (see North Africa) during the period that France was the colonial power there; the urbanization of land traditionally planted with olive trees*; upheavals due to the development of tourism on the Côte d'Azur, and in the countryside around the town of Aix, which used to be the main olive

Olive grove in Les Baux-de-Provence.

producing regions of France; and finally, increased labor costs.

In the aftermath of the Second World War, per capita consumption of olive oil fell steeply. Today, although the demand for olive oil has increased significantly, it still accounts for less than ten percent of total French oil consumption. As a result, a few independent growers and mills* are attempting to revive the sector. The government's policy of subsidies for the cultivation of olive trees (about 5,000 francs per acre) is beginning to have a positive impact, especially in traditional olive growing regions, where the production of olive oil and wine had collapsed. Following the example of Tuscany, a number of French wine growers have decided to embark on the production of high quality olive oil. In all, over 8,000 acres will be planted by the end of 2001. However, a distinctive feature of olive growing France remains its amateur aspect. Out of 20,000 oil producers, only 4,000 are professional growers, a factor that restricts development in the field.

Nyons is the northernmost point in France where olives can be grown successfully. Curiously, the local olive variety*, the *tanche*, not only resists freezing, but seems to thrive on it.

Numerous varieties of olive are cultivated in France. In Corsica, olive oil was traditionally pressed in the spring, from late-ripening olives harvested after being allowed to fall naturally from the tree. This method produces oil with an excellent flavor, but a limited shelf life. In the coming decades, however, Corsica may once again become a land of great growths*.

Red Mullet with Basil and Vallée des Baux Olive Oil

The cuisine of southern France makes abundant use of olive oil, particularly for fish. We asked Jean-André Charial, chef at *L'Oustau de Baumanière* in Les Baux-de-Provence, to give us his excellent recipe for red mullet.

Serves 4
• 8 red mullets
• fish broth (if needed)
• black olives

For the *Pistou* sauce:
• 1 cup Vallée des Baux olive oil
• 1 bouquet garni
• 1 tomato
• ½ teaspoon sherry vinegar
• ½ shallot
• basil

First prepare the sauce (preferably a day or two ahead of time). Scald the tomato with boiling water, so the skin can be easily removed. Use a small paring knife, cut the tomato in half and remove the seeds. Chop the basil and tomato flesh, place in the sherry vinegar and oil with the half shallot (finely chopped), salt, and pepper. Allow to marinate for one or two days. The longer the sauce marinates, the better it will be.

When you purchase the mullets, ask to have them scaled and cleaned. Rinse the fish, and use tweezers to remove the bones. In a non-stick skillet, sauté the fish on both sides, skin-side first, for about three minutes. Or steam them over the broth (skin-side against the basket), also for about three minutes.

Place the marinated tomato on a serving dish and arrange the cooked mullet over it. Remove the pits from the black olives, cut in half, and use as garnish for the fish. Just before serving, pour a spoonful of sauce over the fish.

Accompany with a chilled white wine from the region, such as a Baux-de-Provence.

Strawberry Duo in Olive Oil infused with Vanilla

This recipe is by chef Jacques Chibois, author of *Olive Oil* (Flammarion, 2000). The refined flavor of the oil, the sweet vanilla, and the tart strawberries marry surprisingly well. This recipe proves that olive oil has a place in every course of a meal, from hors d'oeuvres to desserts.

Serves 4
- 2 cups strawberries
- 1 cup wild strawberries
- 3 tablespoons fruity olive oil
- 1 pod vanilla
- 1 lime
- 1 ¼ oz sugar

Halve the vanilla pod. Scrape out the grains and put them in a small cooking pan together with the oil. Cut the pod into fine slivers, and add to the pan. Warm the oil and the vanilla together at a temperature of no more than 120°F (49°C) for three minutes. Remove the oil-vanilla mixture from the heat and leave to infuse in a cool place, away from powerful odors covered with a clean, dry cloth.

Next, wash, dry and hull the strawberries, taking care not to bruise them. (Please note that wild strawberries should not be washed, as they are too fragile.) Arrange the berries on elegant serving plates.

Wash and dry the lime (untreated for preference). Grate the peel very finely. Mix it with the sugar and sprinkle over the strawberries. Add a dash of freshly squeezed lemon or lime juice. To finish off, just before serving, pour the oil and vanilla infusion over the strawberries.

This dish can be served with a scoop of home-made berry sorbet. Cherry and raspberry work very well. It is wonderful outside on a hot summer's day.

Accompany with a chilled, slightly sweet white wine from the region, or with a glass of punch with diced fruit.

Freeze

Freezing weather is the greatest enemy of the olive tree*. If a freeze occurs under conditions of high humidity, olive trees can actually be killed, and in extreme conditions may actually explode. At the very least, the bark will split and leave the tree vulnerable to attack from insects and the "olive knot" bacterium. When such frosts happen, the groves have to be uprooted (an arduous task) and replanted; it takes eight years for them to recover sufficiently to bear fruit again—and even longer for their yield to be profitable. Yet surprisingly, the quality of the olives that can be salvaged after a frost is not necessarily adversely affected.

For many centuries, France* was the country most vulnerable to these catastrophes. On 8 January 1789, a severe cold snap destroyed some eighty percent of the olive trees between the towns of Aix-en-Provence and Tarascon. As the Royal Administrator of Provence noted at the time, "The freezes have been so severe . . . they have destroyed the land's principal resource for years to come." There was another severe frost in 1956 which has a disastrous effect on olive oil production, ruining many formerly prosperous towns. In 1985 it was the turn of Tuscany to suffer a severe freeze. The temperature fell to minus 10°F (minus 25°C). The Arno River froze, and 85 percent of the region's olive trees were destroyed.

Chef Jacques Chibois.

An olive tree killed by the 1956 freeze, Provence.

After such a catastrophe, one can only wonder at the quantities of the popular olive oil produced in Tuscany today. More recently, California suffered in similar conditions during the winter of 1990.

Recent research has shown that the way a tree is cultivated plays a role in its survival of freezing weather. When the tree's canopy is excessively pruned, it loses its natural protection against frost, and well-watered trees are more easliy damaged than those that are watered less frequently after pruning. Another factor is the variety involved. *Ascolano* is the hardiest variety, followed by *Mission, Sevillano*, and *Barouni,* which have all proved fairly resistant to frost in agricultural experiments.

Gastronomy

It would take a separate book to describe all the gastronomic uses of olive oil, that indispensable ingredient in the cuisine of so many Mediterranean countries. Where butter once reigned supreme in the gastronomic pantheon, olive oil is now returning to favor, particularly among the greatest chefs. The Romans of antiquity* were quick to distinguish between olives harvested at different times of year: the bitter oil from late-harvested olives was popular for certain dishes such as dried beans; the milder oil from early-harvested olives preferred for dressing salads. The Romans also established a pressing*

hierarchy, with the cost* of various grades officially set by an edict from the Emperor Diocletian: virgin oil, *olei flos* (prime) was the most expensive, at forty sesterces per unit; second pressing oil, *oleum sequens*, cost twenty-four sesterces; and ordinary oil, *oleum cibarium*, cost only twelve sesterces. Olive oil was sometimes blended with sesame or almond oil. The best quality oil was used in great households as a condiment, combined with vinegar or *garum* (a preserved fish paste popular in Rome and similar, apparently, to the *nuoc mâm* sauce used today in Vietnamese cuisine).

Olive oil was not widely used in Northern Europe until much later. Traditional Celtic cuisine was based on animal fat, especially lard. The olive oil introduced by the Romans was too costly to be popular,

and its use was restricted mainly to frying. It was often associated with visits to the doctor to have one's ears cleaned, which hardly made people want to eat it! In the South, however, olive oil had long been adopted as a flavoring for "oiling" soup or bread. Although olive oil was accused by the medical profession for over half a century of producing "bad" cholesterol, it is recognized today as beneficial to health*, as part of a healthy lifestyle. As a result, it is making a strong comeback on dining tables all over Europe. North America is still somewhat reticent, but Californian olive growers are making efforts to popularize their products. It is such a versatile product, for everything from *hors d'oeuvres* to desserts, that every household should have a bottle handy in the kitchen!

Mezzes prepared by Nicole Lefort: *tapenade*, salads, anchovy paste, squash pie, cod au gratin, tomatoes provençal, chanterelle mushrooms in vinegar, peppers, eggplant, chickpeas, and fresh goat cheese, served with a selection of olive oils.

Olive grove, Crete.

■ GREECE

In Antiquity,* the olive tree* was the emblem of Greece. A gift from Athena to the city that bears her name (see Mythology) and to Attica as a whole, the olive tree remains central to Greek culture today. In Greek Orthodox ritual, consecrated olive oil is used to anoint infants during baptism, to illuminate altars and household icons, and is burned during funerals. The Greeks are the world's leading consumers of olive oil,

accounting for five gallons per capita annually—or, according to ancient texts, about the same amount as 3,000 years ago. Aristotle considered oleiculture a science. According to an ancient proverb, "Bread is a necessity, oil a luxury," and the Greeks prayed to the gods, not only for their daily bread, but also for their daily oil.

In Greece, olive groves cover an area measuring over 1,700,000 acres. The fifth-ranking producer of olive oil worldwide, Greece exports most of its oil, even to other producing countries such as Italy*. Ordinary virgin oil is used primarily in blends marketed under major brand names. Meanwhile, however, producers (notably cooperatives*) that have chosen to develop their own oils and emphasize quality are increasing in number. Olive oil has such a historic—even mystical—resonance in Greece, that consumers expect to enjoy not just oil, but a nectar of the gods!

The cultivation* of olives is ideally suited to the geography and climate* of Greece: proximity to the sea, hills, and mountains, combined with hot summers. However, the remarkable efforts of Greek olive growers serve as a reminder that this tree requires considerable care. The magnificent Greek olive groves are espaliered; drainage and irrigation* is often supplied by windmills that use sea breezes to distribute the moisture needed to protect the soil and nourish the trees. Numerous varieties* are cultivated in Greece: *glykolia, lianolia, liastra, meilolia, striftolia, thrubolia, tsunati,* and so on. The regions most famed for their olive oil are the Pelopennese peninsula and the islands of Lesbos, Samos, Corfu, and Crete.

Olive groves have been grown on Crete longer than anywhere else. Olive trees are everywhere on this island, which boasts no less than 13 million trees, cultivated according to traditional methods, in groves usually owned by individual families. The average size of a Cretan olive grove is about six acres. Olive oil from this island is not ranked highly by connoisseurs, but the recent fad for the "Cretan Diet," especially in the United States, has burnished its image. Is olive oil from Crete more beneficial to the health than others? There is no definitive answer to the question, but the people of Crete, who consume approximately half a cup per capita per day, have the lowest mortality rate due to cardio-vascular disease in the world.

Tarama

Greek cuisine is relatively unpretentious. A deliciously fresh piece of cheese with bread and a dash of olive oil, a bottle of wine, and there you have it: the classic "Greek diet." However, the fame of this dish has circled the globe. A combination of seafood, bread, and olive oil, it perfectly sums up this country's outstanding gastronomic assets.

Serves 4
• 6 to 8 oz smoked cod roe
• 1 slice stale bread
• juice of ½ lemon
• garlic cloves (to taste)
• 1 cup olive oil

Soak the bread in water until soft, then squeeze to extract excess water. Peel and press the garlic cloves.

Remove skin from the cod roe. Blend all ingredients (in a blender, preferably) until perfectly smooth. Serve chilled with country bread or warm toast. Accompany with a white Greek Retsina wine flavored with pine resin, or, if unavailable, with a dry Loire wine, or maybe a great white Burgundy.

Right: A Tuscan
oil, *del Ponte*, and
an oil from
Puglia, *Calogiuri*.

■ GROWTHS
The Best Regions

Despite its noble origins and current popularity, olive oil does not benefit from a classification system as sophisticated at that for wine. France* and Spain* do have "officially guaranteed origin" (AOC) labeling, and in Italy labels may specify the producer's name. But when it comes to olive oil, the

respective traditions of different countries are so varied, it is impossible to give a general definition of the term "growth," or consistent criteria for establishing "guaranteed origin."

In France, oils from the Nyons and Les Baux-de-Provence regions have been awarded AOC status, and conform to extremely strict standards. The AOC label is also expected shortly for oils from Haute-Provence. In Spain there are six official labels of guaranteed origin: Les Garrigues and Siurana in Catalonia; Baena, Priego de Cordoba, Sierra Magina, and Sierra Segura in Andalusia.

Above: An oil
from Puglia,
Tenute de Corato;
a Sardinian oil,
Argiolos Iolao;
and a Tuscan oil,
San Guido.

In Italy, the Tuscany and Umbria labels indicate only that most of the product comes from one of these two administrative regions. The addition of the estate name is a primary indicator of quality: these oils are considered authentic "growths" (see Buyer's Guide).

Some stores have developed a policy of selecting growths on the basis of their origin—for example, Fattorie di Galiga e Vetrice of Tuscany—and make a point of specifying the date of pressing*, which makes it possible to ascertain the (crucial)

freshness of the oil. Some restaurants that feature olive oil in the dishes on their menus also sell growths they have themselves selected, such as the Ligurian Rosmarino oil used at the *Cipriani* in Venice*, or the regional oils offered by restaurants *Le Moulin* in Mougins

Above: AOC
(Origin Officially
Guaranteed) olive
oil from the
Vallée des Baux.

and *l'Oustau de Baumanière* in Les Baux-de-Provence.

Reliable guides to fine olive oils include include *The Olive Oil Companion* by Judy Ridgway, *The Essential Olive Oil Companion* by Anne Dolamore, and *Olive Oil* by Jacques Chibois (see Bibliography). Each of these works presents a selection, with commentary, of one hundred or more fine olive oils, particularly Italian ones.

Olive harvest in Provence.

Following pages: Olive harvest at the Carli grove in Muret, France.

The olives fall into vast nets spread under the trees.

Harvesting

It does not take much imagination to realize how difficult it must be to harvest olives. The fruit is tiny, and, due to the ratio of pit to flesh, huge quantities are required for producing oil. Depending on the region and varieties* of fruit, olives are harvested at different periods of the year: from September-October (green olives), or November (black olives), continuing through January or February.

The ancient Greeks harvested olives by hand—a task often entrusted to women in eastern countries—or shaken off the tree using long poles. The trees' branches can be damaged by poles, however, and in eighteenth-century Provence, this method was banned unless rigorous precautions were taken. Sometimes olives and leaves were pulled off the branches by pickers wearing finger stalls, and fell on large cloths spread under the trees to catch them. The next step was winnowing, or separating the fruit from the leaves and other debris. Today, labor costs represent a major problem for olive growers. They can increase tenfold from one country to another, which explains the dramatic differences in retail prices. Labor currently accounts for some fifty percent of total production costs, compared with about fifteen percent in 1950. Since the end of the Second World War, olives grown in many of the larger groves are harvested using mechanical equipment. A special vibrating machine shakes the olives off the branches and into nets attached beneath. Another machine then sucks the olives up from the nets. To accommodate these machines, the trees must be planted in evenly spaced rows on relatively flat land, and subjected to radical pruning*. Since green olives will not thrive under these conditions, mechanization is only possible for harvesting black olives. In any case, the very best oils are made only from hand-picked olives.

oleum oliue.

Al nature c. ᵹ. ḥ. temperatiᵹ. melius er eo. ... ᵹeñse bonu. Iuuamentum. inpinguat ᵹ cito ᵹesenᵒis. nocumentum. aberat stomacum ᵹ conuertatur. remotio nocumen. m... in fra fercula.

The Olive-Oil Vendor. Miniature from *Tacuinum Sanitatis,* Lombardy, fourteenth century. Bibliothèque Nationale de France, Paris.

■ Health

Unlike other commonly used oils, which are extracted by refining* (i.e. industrial processing), olive oil extracted by simple cold pressing* retains components in suspension, which chemists call "unsaponifiable"—that is, the particles which give olive oil its therapeutic properties. These pigments, vitamins, and antioxidants act effectively to prevent cardio-vascular disease and retard the signs of aging. Olive oil is rich in oleic acid, also beneficial to the health.

Olive oil, once considered a gift of the gods (see Religion; Symbolism), was used as an ointment* in antiquity*. Galen, the Greek doctor who devised the theory of the humors, discovered the beneficial effects of olive oil taken internally for treating the liver and gall bladder, and particularly for the prevention of gall stones. Scientists have subsequently proved that olive oil does indeed regulate the secretion of bile. Recent discoveries have shown that olive oil's virtues extend also to the digestive and intestinal processes (peristalsis). At the end of the nineteenth century, the scientists Ewald and Boas proved that olive oil increases the alkaline secretion of the stomach's mucous membranes. More recently, scientists have demonstrated that olive oil can prevent the formation of gastric ulcers: olive oil stimulates secretion of a digestive hormone, cholecystocinine.

More recently still, statistical studies on diet and health conducted by universities in France and the United States have raised olive oil to an exalted rank. The famous Cretan diet, rich in olive oil and red wine, is now thought to explain the low rate of cancer and cardio-vascular disease on the island and the enviable longevity of its inhabitants. Whether or not this will be borne out by further research, physicians are unanimous in praising the benefits of olive oil in the fight against "bad" cholesterol.

▉ Irrigation

The olive tree* thrives in warm, Mediterranean-type climates. This does not mean, however, that it can do without water.

In antiquity*, the problem was solved by "earthing" the tree (surrounding the base of its trunk with earth to retain the moisture); by laying bare the roots of the tree and forming a sort of funnel around them to collect moisture; or by installing irrigation pipes— a skill for which the ancient Greeks and Romans were famous.

Modern technology has made it easier to control the flow of water more efficiently, thus improving productivity. On flat land (rare in the Mediterranean regions), irrigation by gravity can be achieved through a network of trenches and water collection pools. The one drawback of this simple and economical method (for which no heavy equipment is required) is the amount of water that is lost: much of it evaporates in the sun.

The most commonly practiced method is the sprinkling system, also used for other crops. However, this method is costly in terms of both equipment (the sprinklers) and labor, and requires more water than is generally available in olive-growing regions*. The current trend is therefore toward piped irrigation. Irrigation pipes cost only half as much as sprinkling systems and also have the advantage of being able to deliver fertilizer along with the water. The system is complex, since it involves laying pipes throughout the olive grove, and the water must be filtered in order to prevent the formation of silt deposits in the pipes; but it uses thirty percent less water than traditional sprinkling systems.

■ ITALY

Italian olive oils are considered the best in the world. The first Italian olive trees were probably planted in Sicily, before spreading throughout virtually the entire country, with the sole exception of the northern Piedmont and Aosta Valley regions. In Antiquity*, both the Romans and the Greeks venerated the olive tree* and developed extremely sophisticated techniques for cultivation, especially in irrigation*, and for oil extraction, using a system of winch pressing*. The Italians have always been discriminating connoisseurs of olive oil. Although they consume less than the Greeks, they are very keen on buying quality oils. Olive oil is interwoven with the country's social structure, since aristocratic families traditionally produced their own wine and olive oil on the estates surrounding their country villas.

Italy, which ranks third in the world after Spain* and Tunisia (see North Africa) in olive grove acreage (with some 2.5 million acres under cultivation), produces most of the world's premium oils. From the Alpine lakes to arid Sicily, the country is geographically diverse, producing olive growths as varied as the soil and climate of each respective region. The pale yellow oils of Trentino and Lombardy are mild and subtle; those of Venezia a little fruitier. Umbrian oil is suave and relatively neutral—a quality sometimes sought after in cooking—whereas the oils of Puglia, Calabria, and Sicily burst with fragrance and aroma. Although less subtle than others, they are also less costly. But the two most highly prized regions are indisputably Liguria and Tuscany.

Olive oil from Imperia, in Liguria, is one of the best in Italy. Terraced olive groves surround this fief of oleiculture, and its finest growth, Primoruggiu, is a non-filtered oil prized throughout the world. Three other

Olive grove, Tuscany.

oils from Liguria are especially famous: Vallaurea from the Oneglia Valley; Fructus, very fruity, as indicated by its name; and Biancardo, pressed in the spring from a late-ripening variety* called *taggiashe*.

The Tuscans are generally believed to produce the best wines, the best fragrances . . . and the best olive oils. The explosion in tourism experienced by this region has spread its fame throughout the world. As a result of the disastrous 1985 freeze* that destroyed eighty-five percent of the olive trees in Tuscany, most of today's groves are new plantations and modest in size, but all growers are obsessed with the quest for excellence. The areas of Lucca, Grossetto, and Arezzo are the most illustrious. Here, olive groves surround sometimes luxurious villas, which makes a trip along the Olive Oil Route an incomparable delight. The star of the

region is Laudemio, an AOC (Origin Officially Guaranteed) label created by some fifty growers aiming for peerless quality. This noble oil is green in color and crisp on the palate, with none of the overwhelming strength of oils from the South.

In Italy, as in the other countries bordering the Mediterranean, olive oil has pride of place in its gastronomy*. The repertoire of its uses is immense, from *pasta olio-alio* (with oil and garlic) to the Neapolitan pizzas that should be sprinkled with this oil and no other.

Note that some olive estates also offer overnight stays (the Ravidà estate in Sicily, the Villa dei Barbi near Siena), or have their own restaurants (the *Don Alfonso*, facing the Isle of Capri) or hotels (Il Bottacio di Montignoso, an old Tuscan mill). All offer pleasant and gastronomically delectable country holidays.

Venetian Carpaccio

Carpaccio, a recent invention, is a simple dish composed of thinly sliced raw beef (sometimes veal) dipped in olive oil and served with grated Parmesan cheese. Our own preference is for the original recipe as first created by Giuseppe Cipriani (founder of the hotel that bears his name, and of Harry's Bar in Venice*) and still prepared exactly the same way at the restaurant of the Cipriani Hotel.

Serves 4
• 1 pound tenderloin steak
• yolk of 1 egg
• juice of 1 lemon
• olive oil

The most important ingredient is the meat: it must be prime quality and lightly marbled with fat. Cut the raw meat into paper-thin slices. Arrange the slices on a plate, and top with a classic mayonnaise made with the egg yolk, olive oil, and lemon juice. Season to taste with salt and pepper. The mayonnaise may also be used for

decorating the outer edge of the plate. Accompany with a Venezia Merlot or, if not available, with a Faugères (Château Grezan) or Saint-Chinian (Château Cazals-Viel), which are similar to their Italian counterparts.

Lamp

Familiar since antiquity*, oil lamps were for many centuries the primary source of lighting—particularly in the Middle and Far East—since they are more easily carried than candles. In Europe, oil lamps acquired an aura of romance following the success of the story "Aladdin, or the Marvelous Lamp," from *The Arabian Nights* (translated in the eighteenth century). In the nineteenth century, lighting oil was replaced by kerosene; then shortly thereafter (1836), by acetylene gas; and, finally (1879), by electricity.

The lamps used in Ancient Greece for the illumination of temples were sometimes huge. The golden lamp dedicated to Athena (*see* Mythology) on the Acropolis, designed by sculptor and goldsmith Callimachus (fifth century B.C.) had a reservoir holding some eight gallons of oil, and could burn day and night for a year. Muslims and Greek Orthodox Christians used (and still use) oil-burning lamps for ecclesiastical rites celebrating the major turning points in life: birth, marriage, death. Light is a sign of the divine, as opposed to the darkness where evil reigns. The Koran states: "God is the light of heaven and earth. His light is like a niche in the wall holding a lamp ... it burns with the oil of a sacred tree, the olive tree*, which is neither of the East nor of the West, and this oil burns, and the brightness of its light shines, without fire."

Modern oil lamps (like those of the past) are fueled with a poor quality olive oil called lamp oil, which is refined from the third pressing* or from olive cakes.

Oil lamp with a seven-branch candlestick, discovered at Volubilis. Archeological Museum, Rabat, Morocco.

■ Literature

The role played by the olive tree* in literature reflects its relative importance to local economies. We thus find a host of references to it in the literature of Greece and the Italian peninsula from antiquity* to the present, and in authors such as Shakespeare and Henry James. Sophocles (496–406 B.C.) praises the olive tree in his play *Œdipus at Colonus*: "There is a peerless tree, unmatched either on the soil of Asia or on that of the Isle of Pelops, an indomitable tree, one that is reborn from itself, a plant that arrests the enemy weapon, that grows stronger here than in any other clime: that tree is the olive tree. Its foliage is brilliant, it nourishes our children, and no one, young or old, would ever willfully destroy or harm it!"

The *Iliad* and *Odyssey* contain numerous references to this tree that was sacred to the Ancients. Virgil (70–19 B.C.) celebrates the olive tree in his *Georgics*, and Ovid (43 B.C.–17 A.D.) describes Baucis preparing a celestial meal with olive oil in the *Metamorphoses*. Horace, Lucretius, and Martial also paid tribute to the olive tree. In *Caesar*, Plutarch (c. 49–125 A.D.) notes the importance of the famous general's conquest of Numidia, a land rich in olive oil.

Shepherd Transformed into an Olive Tree. Engraving by Jean Matheus for Ovid's *Metamorphoses*, Paris, 1619. Bibliothèque des Arts décoratifs, Paris.

Édouard Bernard Debat-Ponsan, *Le Massage*, 1883. Oil on canvas. Musée des Augustins, Toulouse.

Closer to our own time, the Italian poet Gabriele D'Annunzio (1863–1938) composed a lyric ode to the olive tree:
Olive trees, sacred trees, O! you who in the torrid southern heat, attentive, harken to the sea, O! you who harken to its mysterious word in the splendor of the firmaments, Olive trees, sacred trees, hear the prayer of man ... pour forth the peace shining from within you, your glorious peace, pour it forth benignly unto my heart!

The olive tree has also been popular in Northern European literature. Its role as a symbol of peace appears frequently: "I bring no overture of war, no taxation of homage: I hold the olive in my hand; my words are as full of peace as matter." (Shakespeare, *Twelfth Night*).

■ Massage
Olive oil of inferior quality was once used primarily for massages. The Greeks and Egyptians of antiquity* massaged their

skin with olive oil to protect and soften it after bathing, and to relax and warm up the muscles and ligaments before (and during) athletic events. The old traditional ayurvedic massage still practiced in India also uses olive oil, which is imported and relatively expensive. This custom is a thousand years old and probably originated in Asia Minor.

For massages, olive oil is usually used pure, but essential oils may be added to enhance its therapeutic effect (see Health).

Thanks to its cosmetic* properties, olive oil can also be used daily during the morning shower. After soaping, olive oil is massaged gently over the wet body, followed by a second soaping and rinsing. If a subtler scent is desired for these massages, the olive oil may be blended with the oil impregnated with Chinese anise, fennel, bergamot, etc. In the Far East, olive oil is also used for scalp massages, to add shine to the hair.

■ MIDDLE EAST

Olive oil's popularity can be traced to the Middle East (see Antiquity). Although the olive tree* is not widely cultivated in Iran or Iraq (12,000 and 25,000 acres of olive groves, respectively), the production of olive oil remains a major industry around the Mediterranean Sea: in Syria (nearly one million acres), Lebanon (80,000 acres), Palestine and Israel (250,000 acres). The oil produced in these regions comes primarily from the *barnea, manzanillo, nabali,* and *suri* varieties*.

Israel produces olive oils of high quality, mainly in Galilee. The traditional importance of the olive tree in Judaic culture (see Religion) should be underscored. In the Book of Judith, this tree symbolizing vigor, beauty, and fertility is elected king. The land of Israel is called "a land of oil olive, and honey" (Deuteronomy, 8:8). The oldest surviving vestiges of olive wood were discovered in Israel and date from 42,900 B.C. Olive wood was employed in the region during prehistoric times, and the "blocks" used before the invention of the olive press appeared during the Neolithic era (8,300 B.C.).

Wild olive trees were gradually replaced by cultivated groves, which spread throughout ancient Israel in the second half of the fourth millennium B.C., at the edge of the Golan forest and along the coast. In this area, archeologists have discovered the earliest mortars for crushing olives—a pressing* technique that undoubtedly produced an oil of excellent quality, comparable to the *fleur d'olive* (premium) oil today. The city of Saida in Lebanon was once called Sidon, a name derived from the Hebrew word *zeitun*, or olive tree (from which the word *azeite*, "olive" in both Portuguese and Spanish, is also derived). However, the wars that periodically ravage this part of the world have not spared the olive tree*. In Lebanon, which has been gripped by civil war ever since 1975, most of the olive groves in the southern part of the country and on the plain of Bekaa have been destroyed. Disease and parasites*—particularly the olive fly—have proliferated in these semi-abandoned olive groves and yields have dropped dramatically. Even today, with peace restored and a strong rise in the demand for olive oil worldwide, Lebanon still has not managed to re-establish its former levels of production. In Syria, however, relative political stability and the absence of tourist traffic along the coast have favored the tradition of a balanced cultivation* of olive trees.

At present, Middle Eastern olive oils

Olive grove in Samaria, Israel.

do not have a strong reputation for quality and are therefore relatively unknown outside their home markets. On the other hand, the gastronomy* of Syria and Lebanon is universally appreciated, thanks to a diaspora and restaurants opened in major cities all over the world. Olive oil now rivals sesame oil in the preparation of some classic dishes: taboulé, humus (a purée of chickpeas and oil), *kébbé* (meat balls made with ground lamb mixed with bulgur, onion, and parsley), eggplant caviar, and so on.

Goat Cheese Fondue

Goat cheese is the constant companion to olive oil throughout the Mediterranean. In this recipe, fresh goat cheese is heated briefly in the oven and served accompanied by croutons rubbed with garlic. This delectably aromatic dish is ideal at aperitif time or as an hors d'œuvre.

Serves 4
• 4 goat cheeses
• thyme
• small squares of stale bread
• garlic
• olive oil

Rub the bread with garlic and fry in olive oil until golden. Place the cheeses briefly in the oven

until partially melted. Sprinkle the cheese with thyme flavored olive oil and serve surrounded by the croutons, which can be dipped in the softened cheese. This dish goes well with Ouzo, chilled Pastis, or a good rosé that has been thoroughly chilled.

Olive mill in Callian, France.

Woman on the Island of Crete.

Mills

Olive mills have existed since antiquity*, although for many centuries they had to compete with manual olive oil production in the home. Under the feudal system, liege lords exercised a monopoly over the tools used for processing olive oil. As late as the eighteenth century, growers were still forced to press their olives at the "communal" mill, i.e. the one controlled by the local lord. The lord exacted a tribute amounting to one-twentieth of the oil and of the crushed olive residue, which could be used for a second pressing*. The Industrial Revolution eventually did away with these feudal privileges, opening the way to the creation of privately owned mills.

However, the traditional conflict of interest between pressers and growers remained unresolved. A fresh turning point came in the early twentieth century with the introduction of cooperatives*. Independent olive mills were forced to bring their prices down to the levels practiced by the cooperatives. Such conflicts as exist now are those which pitch producers against dealers, while the mills act merely as technical sub-contractors.

Today, olive mills have become increasingly creative, "designing" premium oils and opening their presses to tourists in much the same way that vintners open their châteaux (see Address Book). There is now healthy competition among mills, reflecting a desire to

improve the already high level of quality—like wine, the best oils are labeled *cru**. Mills also enhance their brand image through the direct marketing of oil and derivative products. They monitor both the quality of the olives they use and each step involved in the production process (*see* Crushing; Pressing) in order to obtain oil with an acid content of less than one percent—the standard for the "Extra Virgin" label—or one that could one day earn the AOC (Origin Officially Guaranteed) label. Top quality is achieved through one of two methods: either by pressing extremely fresh olives immediately after harvesting*, in order to obtain oil with a "crisp" aroma featuring leafy and green apple notes; or by storing the olives until they have become overripe, in order to obtain oil with an aroma that is more mature and full bodied, long on the palate, with notes of woodland and prune.

Mills may also create blends using different varieties* of olive. If they also own the grove, they can select which varieties to plant in order to obtain the best balance for their blends.

■ Mount of Olives

The Mount of Olives, a hill near Jerusalem, was the scene of a number of major events in the life of Jesus Christ, who often went there to pray and to preach: it was there that he foretold the destruction of Jerusalem. He was arrested by the Temple guards at the foot of the Mount, in the Garden of Gethsemane (*Gat Shemen*, or "olive press," in Hebrew). According to Saint Luke, Christ's Ascension forty days

after his Resurrection occurred at the summit of this hill. Christ's final prayer and arrest are, after the Crucifixion, the episodes most frequently illustrated by painters (see Art). Among the famous artists who have portrayed these scenes are Andrea Mantegna, Raphael, Titian, Rubens, and Delacroix. The Mount of Olives was designated a major holy site for

the Christian religion* during the Byzantine era: by the sixth century, no less than twenty-four churches had been built there. Later, the crusaders erected an octagonal church on the spot where the Ascension is thought to have occurred, and pilgrims journeyed there in order to worship on the ground where Christ once walked. The Mount of Olives, near the Temple, is also important to Judaism: it is here, according to scripture, that the quick and the dead will assemble on the Final Judgment Day, and the dead buried on the slopes of the hill will be the first to be resurrected. This historic and sacred spot is open to strollers today, and olive trees still grow in the Garden of Gethsemane.

Eugène Delacroix, *Christ in the Olive Garden*, 1824–27. Oil on canvas. Church of Saint Paul and Saint Louis, Paris.

75

Poseidon and Athena Competing for the Domination of Attica. Cameo, Hellenistic Era. Museo Archeologico Nazionale, Naples.

■ Mythology

The olive plays a central role in the mythologies of many cultures, but it inspired the Greeks to the greatest heights of all. The legend recounting the origin of Athens explains the pre-eminence of the olive tree as a result of competition between Poseidon and Athena for possession of Attica. Zeus decreed that the land would be attributed to the god proposing the single creation most useful to humankind. Poseidon proposed the horse; Athena the olive tree. After due deliberation, the assembled gods decided that humans had more to gain from the oil-rich fruit of the olive tree, and Athena won the day. In gratitude to their goddess and protector, the Greeks founded the city of Athens and planted the first olive tree in the Erechtheum, the

temple of Athena and Poseidon. The olive tree appears twice in the *Labors of Hercules*. First, the hero thrusts his huge cudgel (made of olive wood, naturally) into the ground and a grove of fine olive trees immediately springs up. Second, having accomplished the tasks imposed by Hera, Hercules returns to Mount Olympus with shoots from his olive trees and promises to plant a grove in gratitude to the gods for their clemency. At Ephesus, under the shade of an olive tree, there was a sacred spring named Ypelaio. It is here that Leto is said to have given birth to Apollo and Artemis—although the same myth sometimes mentions the Isle of Delos … and a palm tree. The ancient Egyptians believed that Isis, the "universal mother," was responsible for teaching humans how to extract oil from olives.

Merry Joseph Blondel, *Neptune and Minerva Disputing Control of Athens*, 1822. Oil on canvas. Musée du Louvre, Paris.

■ NORTH AFRICA

The countries along the North African coast have possessed olive groves since the earliest eras of recorded history. In the *Aeneid*, Virgil described the founding of Carthage in 814 B.C. by Dido and the Phoenicians, who brought currency, alphabet, numbers, and the olive tree* to this part of the world—in other words, the main attributes of advanced civilization. The Carthaginian colonizers built a vast commercial empire based primarily on its abundant supply of olive oil. North Africa's major problem has always been the area's arid climate. However, the practice of dry farming (in Tunisia called *baali*, a term derived from the Phoenician god Baal) was already working miracles in Antiquity*. Even when supplied with little water, the Carthaginian olive trees were so productive, the Ancients described them as *milliari*, or capable of producing thousands of fruits. When Caesar conquered Carthage, one of his objectives was to control the production of oil. In his *Memoirs*, he reports that he forced the city of Leptis to pay an annual tribute of 300,000 pounds of olive oil in return for its alliance with Juba. The Romans introduced irrigation, which resulted in significantly higher yields. They also modernized oil extraction and storage techniques, and developed types of grafting that had never been used before.

Carthage fell to the Arabs in 698 A.D. The newcomers were unfamiliar with the olive tree, and allowed the great olive groves to lie fallow. It was not until the arrival of the Arabian Moors, expelled from Andalusia following the conquest of Grenada (1492), that this valuable resource was exploited once

more. Since then, the cultivation* of olive trees has developed steadily. Olives are now a major crop in North Africa, especially in Tunisia. In this country, direct heir to ancient Carthage, there were seven million olive trees in 1900, twelve million in 1920, and twenty-seven million at independence in 1956. There are sixty million today.

Tunisia currently ranks second worldwide in olive oil production and exports. Its specialty is an oil of ordinary quality, used in blends marketed under European brands, with a distinctive flavor that has ensured its enduring success. The cost* of this Tunisian oil remains highly competitive, due to the exemplary modernization of growing and processing methods, and also to low labor costs. Compared with the olive groves in Tunisia, which cover almost four million acres, those of neighboring countries are less spectacular but not

Olive grove, Cap Bon (Tunisia).

insignificant: almost one million acres in Morocco; 500,000 in Algeria; 250,000 in Libya; and over 60,000 in Egypt. Olive oil is an omnipresent feature of North African cuisine, particularly in Tunisia and Morocco.

The Tunisians' predilection for fish, and their skill in preparing it, make the little restaurants along the coast havens of gastronomy*. The subtle aroma and tart flavor of the local olive oils is ideal in combination with seafood.

Mussels with Chopped Tomatoes and Saffron Oil

Saffron is a favorite with the Arabs. It is an ideal partner for olive oil, also used in Andalusian paella and Milanese risotto.

Serves 4
- 4 pounds mussels in the shell
- 1½ cups skinned and chopped ripe tomatoes
- bay leaf
- 3–4 strands saffron
- juice of 1 lemon
- pepper
- 9 tablespoons olive oil

Place the saffron in the lemon juice and allow to steep overnight. The next day, scald and peel the tomatoes, remove seeds, and chop. Scrub and trim the mussels. Place 4 tablespoons of olive oil in a large casserole, add the chopped tomatoes and bay leaf, sauté for 5 minutes. Add the mussels, cover, and shake over high heat until the mussels open (4–5 minutes). Remove upper shells from mussels and arrange on serving plates. Dot with the tomatoes, add pepper to taste. Strain the lemon juice, discard the saffron. Add 5 tablespoons olive oil to the lemon juice, blend, and pour a few drops of this mixture on each mussel. Serve lukewarm. Accompany with a local Tunisian white wine or a dry, fruity Bordeaux.

◼ Ointment

Ointments have figured prominently in folk medicine from Antiquity* to the present day. Once used primarily for healing wounds, they were often based on olive oil, with the addition of various spices and therapeutic agents.

In Antiquity, the greatest "composer" of ointments—after Hippocrates, Pliny, and Galen—was Dioscorides, also called Pelanius (first century A.D.). This Greek botanist wrote an important treatise on the therapeutic properties of over six hundred plants, and his formulas have survived throughout the intervening centuries. He recommended using green olive oil as a base for various ointments. His bay oil ointment (made from bay berries and leaves) warms and dilates the pores of the skin, and reduces pain. His rose petal ointment helps to heal wounds and soothes menstrual cramps.

Resin, wax, beef suet, and myrrh were added to olive oil for other healing ointments, as was *cereato de Turnes* (wax, calamine stone, and olive oil). Iris root, powdered and blended with olive oil, cleanses wounds, softens and removes the scabs caused by cauterizing, eases childbirth, and soothes the pain of hemorrhoids. The Arab doctor and philosopher Avicenna recommended an ointment containing olive oil and rosemary blossoms for which he claimed rejuvenating powers.

◼ Olive Tree

Fossilized olive leaves have been found in geological strata dating from the Pleistocene epoch (six million years ago) at Mongardino in Italy*, and the remains of

OLIVIER.
Olea Europaea, L.

olive trees from the late Paleolithic epoch (200,000 years ago) in North Africa*. The wild olive—from which all cultivated varieties are derived—probably originated in Asia Minor, growing in thick forests extending to Anatolia and Greece*. Other hypotheses place its origin in Nubia (lower Egypt), the Atlas Mountains, or Ethiopia. In any case, it is definitely native to the Mediterranean Basin, where it has become the emblem for the entire area. Olive trees were first cultivated six thousand years ago (see Antiquity) in Asia Minor, and the oldest olive

Left: *Ointment container in the form of a Nubian slave with jar, circa* 1350 B.C. Egyptian Museum, Cairo.

81

customarily pruned to a height of six feet or so, to facilitate harvesting*. In some older groves, especially in Greece, they are allowed to grow higher, but seldom exceed thirty feet. The tree generally begins to yield appreciable quantities of fruit in its eighth year and can continue to yield until it reaches 100 years of age. Indeed, some centuries-old trees still produce acceptable yields. The olive tree is capable of adapting to a wide variety of soils. It grows on both siliceous and calcareous sediment. The only soils unsuited to it are those with a high clay content. On the other hand, it must be protected from the wind, which can cause significant losses when the tree is in blossom or the fruit is maturing. Soils which are too humid, whether because they are close to the water table or because they are poorly drained, are not suitable, nor are damp climates*, which foster the development of disease (see Parasites). The olive tree cannot survive freezing temperatures below 15°F (minus 10°C).

■ Packaging

Following the pressing* and decantation processes, olive oil is stored on the production site before embarking on its perilous journey to the consumer. The standards specified by the International Olive Oil Council (see Classification) are especially strict when it comes to packaging. Olive oil is a vulnerable product, and its quality can deteriorate quickly. When packaged improperly, it can absorb undesirable odors and even become a fertile medium for the development

Above and preceding page: *Olea Europa* (common olive tree). Engravings after Pierre Jean Turpin, nineteenth century. Bibliothèque des Arts décoratifs, Paris.

Right: Can of olive oil from Provence.

pits found in Spain* date from the Bronze Age (four thousand years ago).
The wild olive, like the ash and the lilac, belong to the botanical genus *Oleaceae*. It draws nourishment through a root system extending from six inches to five feet beneath the surface of the soil. Its branches grow horizontally two to three times longer than they do vertically. The structure of the trunk depends on the system of pruning* used. In Spain* olive trees with several trunks are common, a rare phenomenon elsewhere. Olive trees are

Metal oil cruets.

of toxic bacteria. Unlike wine, it does not improve with age. Freshness is therefore of prime importance. On the other hand, when it solidifies at low temperatures (due to its glycerin content) this will not affect its quality in any way. The packaging's main role is to protect the oil from air, heat, and light (see Storage). Glass containers are better than plastic, and tinted glass specifically treated to filter ultra-violet rays, or wrapped in a reflective covering (aluminum, tinfoil) insulating the oil from light is best of all. However, the ideal packaging for olive oil is the metal tin, such as those used in the Iberian countries for both ordinary and extra virgin oils. Unfortunately, consumers (mistakenly) shun oil in metallic containers because of its "canned" appearance.

The date the oil was packaged should be inscribed on the outside of the bottle or can. This information is not a sufficient guarantee of freshness, however, since the oil may have been subjected to a lengthy period of storage between processing and packaging. Ideally, the actual pressing date should also be specified.

Parasites

As with all of nature's treasures, the olive tree* is vulnerable to attack, notably by insects. In Antiquity*, growers were already fighting predators which invaded the trees' roots. Columella advised spreading lees of olive oil around the foot of the trees, a procedure that also fertilized the soil. Potash and tallow were used for the same purpose. The worms that feed on the trees' sap and suck it dry were once killed by dripping a vinegar solution on them with a pipette—one by one!

Today we have insecticides and fungicides to deal with the diverse and unrelenting pests that attack olive trees. First comes the miner moth, a caterpillar that feeds on new buds in March and April. It is followed by leaf parasites: the cycloconium, for example, which deposits a brown substance on the leaves and is eradicated with the solution of copper sulfate and lime known as "Bordeaux mixture." Summer ushers in the black cochineal and the olive fly, both of which feed on new fruit. Olive trees are also subject to diseases such as fumagine, which causes a black scale to form on the tree; and psylla, white globules deposited on the olives by a plant louse. The most devastating of all is the olive fly; efforts are currently underway to eradicate it by sterilizing the male flies. Other methods are used in this unending struggle: for example, yellow cardboard covered with bird lime will attract flies (who are partial to yellow) and kill them. With the development of organic agriculture, attempts are also being made to introduce natural olive fly predators in order to bring this terrible plague to an end.

▩ Pesto

Pesto is a condiment combining basil, finely chopped garlic, and olive oil: the three signature ingredients of Mediterranean gastronomy*. The recipe for *pesto*—used to add a crisp, cool touch to hot pasta dishes—can also include parsley, crushed marjoram, and grated Parmesan cheese. *Pesto* originated in Genoa and so, perhaps, did minestrone, which is a close cousin of the Provençal version, *soupe au pistou*. This soup is made with various vegetables (dried red and white beans, fresh green beans, zucchini, carrots, turnips) and small pieces of pasta, to which is added a mixture of chopped tomato, garlic, basil leaves and Parmesan cheese blended in a mortar with olive oil. The characteristic ingredient of all these preparations is basil, a highly aromatic herb. The best basil is the long-leaved type found primarily in Italy*. Although nothing can really replace *pistou* or *pesto* made with fresh ingredients just before serving, they have now become so popular worldwide that they are sold ready made in jars.

■ PORTUGAL

Portugal, with over 740,000 acres of olive groves under cultivation, is the one of the world's leading olive oil producers, and the country has turned the olive tree* (and its oil) into a sort of national emblem. As a main participant in the conquest of the Americas, Portugal played a crucial role in the export of olive oil to the New World: even today, Portuguese oil still dominates the South American market.

Olive groves have been cultivated in the Alentejo region* of Portugal since Antiquity*, and developed significantly under Arab rule. According to legend, when Wamba, the Visigoth sovereign of the Iberian peninsula, was informed of his election to the monarchy, he brandished an olive wood rod and declared, "Only if the rod I hold is transformed into a tree will I follow you!" He then thrust the rod into the ground, whereupon it immediately put forth flowering branches. The Oliveira (Olive Tree) Abbey was subsequently erected on the spot where the miracle is said to have occurred, and "Oliveira" is today one of the most common surnames in Portugal. In the fifteenth century Portugal expanded its merchant navy and its network of trading posts around the world. In the following century, it was able to wrest domination of the oriental spice trade, and also the olive oil and wine trade, from Venice*. Today, olive production in the northern provinces of Tras-Os-Montes, Beira Alta, and Beira Baixa frequently outstrips that in the southern provinces of Ribatejo and Alentejo. Top quality Portuguese oils include those from Quinta da Romaneira in the province of Douro Litoral (in the north), and Mirandela and Moura (north and center).

The Portuguese olive oil industry was in a state of gradual decline when measures were finally taken to restructure it on the basis of improved quality, notably through a system of AOC (Origin Officially Guaranteed) labeling following the Spanish* model. Small groves, cultivated using traditional methods, have a limited yield but often produce quality oils that are naturally organic. Portuguese olive oils, highly competitive in cost*, are beginning to make a dent on the international market. Portuguese gastronomy* is not as familiar to the rest of the world as it should be. Olive oil is used in preference to any other kind, and the country's classic dishes are based on shellfish and seafood. One example is the perennial favorite *bacalhau* (cod), for which olive oil is the essential ingredient. Olive oil is still a feature of local cuisine in Brazil, a former Portuguese colony, and there are a few productive olive groves in the southern part of that country.

Olive grove, Douro Valley (Portugal).

Bacal-hau with Green Apples

Portuguese olive oil sometimes has a strong green apple note, ideal for this light version of the Portuguese national dish based on cod.

Serves 4
- 1 pound salt cod (*bacalhau*)
- 3 green apples
- 5 new potatoes
- 2 cloves garlic, chopped
- a handful of black olives
- 3 onions
- 3 bay leaves
- parsley
- olive oil

Soak the cod overnight, changing the water several times.

The next day: drain the cod, place in a pot with the bay leaves, cover with cold water. Heat to just below the boiling point. Remove from heat and allow to rest for ten minutes.

Preheat oven to 375°F (190°C).

Peel and slice the onions. Slice the potatoes, unpeeled. Remove the core and seeds from the apples and slice, unpeeled. Sauté these ingredients in olive oil. When cooked, arrange in an ovenproof pan. Drain the cod, cut into pieces, and mix with the apples and vegetables. Add the garlic, olives, and parsley. Salt and pepper to taste. Place in oven and bake for five minutes. Sprinkle with fresh olive oil and serve.

This dish is delicious with rice, accompanied by the famous Portuguese *vinho verde* (green wine), a young and very dry Burgundy, or a Languedoc.

Screw press,
Alziari mill, Nice.

PRESSING
An Ancestral Art

Most of the olive oil on the market is labeled "first cold pressing." And pressing, in fact, is the simplest, most widespread, and oldest method of extracting oil from olives. First, the fresh olives are reduced to a paste through crushing*. This initial step also separates the pits from the flesh. Next, the paste is pressed in order to extract the oil. There are two methods of pressing, one modern and one ancient. The ancient method is still used by numerous small producers.

A truly rudimentary procedure is to fill woolen bags with the crushed olives, and then, using ropes, to twist the bags until the oil is extracted. A slightly more advanced but still ancient method calls for placing the olive paste in scurtins, or large flat, round baskets. Scurtins can be made of alfa (in North Africa*), hemp, or esparto in Greece*; today these are often replaced by nylon. The baskets are filled with the olive paste either mechanically or manually (in smaller mills), and then transported to the press. There are several models of ancient olive presses: the quoin-press, with which pressure is exerted by inserting wedges between the pressing block and base; the shaft-press (used in ancient Rome), with a counterweight and windlass, both fragile and difficult to manipulate; and, lastly, the screw-press, the earliest known example of which dates from the first century B.C. This type, also used for grapes, was gradually improved, and until recently was still used in Portugal*.

Men Operating a Screw Press. Fragment of bas-relief. Archeological Museum, Aquilleia, Italy.

The nineteenth century witnessed the development of the hydraulic press, the continuous press, and the centrifuge. The centrifuge is the one used most widely by modern mills*. When this method is used, the olives must be meticulously crushed during the initial step in the process, and they are sometimes sent through a splitter to remove the pits. The resulting paste is then homogenized in a blender, and the extracted liquid placed in a centrifuge decanter that separates the oil from fluid and residue. In former times, the decantation step was not executed mechanically; the paste was simply allowed to rest until the oil, lighter than the other two components, rose to the surface. So-called "pure" oil, or that obtained following the first decantation, is sometimes marketed as is, and will have a cloudy appearance (which has no effect on its quality) and stronger flavor. Most often, however, decanted oil is filtered in order to obtain a more visually appealing golden, translucent product. During the final step, the oil is either bottled or stored in vats. It takes about eleven pounds of olives to produce one quart of oil. *Fleur d'huile* (prime oil) is oil that has been allowed to drain naturally following the first pressing.

Following double page: stone olive press, third century B.C. Haaretz Museum, Tel Aviv.

▪ Pruning

Like all fruit trees, olive trees must be pruned. Methods vary depending on the varieties* and the time of year. The Romans of Antiquity* pruned their olive trees once every eight years. In the nineteenth century, Abbot Rozier advised pruning every two to four years, in March or April. Today, pruning is carried out annually, if possible, between February and May to obtain a maximum yield.

Due to the distinctive features of the olive tree, pruning is particularly important. The growing period for branches lasts from April through late October, but slows during August because of the heat and scarcity of water at that time of the year. The trees are dormant

Above:
Pruning olive
trees,
San Giminiano,
Tuscany.

Left:
Olive grove near
Fez, Morocco.

from November to January, when budding begins. This extremely early budding means that the fruit does not grow on the new wood (which does not develop until April), but on that of the previous year. This is why the tree produces fruit only once every two years. It is almost as if olives trees lacked the energy to grow both branches and fruit in one and the same year, and thus alternate the two activities.

There are three types of pruning, each with its own purpose. Trees are pruned in order to give them shape and a balanced structure. This is a light pruning, done with pruning shears. The goal is to obtain a trunk measuring about three feet high, and to stimulate the growth of main branches at different heights on the trunk. Ideally branches should be of identical length (about one to two feet long) at three different levels on the trunk. Once the tree has attained the desired shape, it is then pruned to stimulate the production of fruit. During this second stage, pruning starts at the center of the tree and works outwards, in order to balance the growth of branches and placement of the fruit. Olive trees must be radically pruned so that the light will penetrate and the fruits will be as near as possible to the trunk, facilitating growth. Branches that bore fruit the previous year are cut back, but the ends of the branches on the third level are retained.

The third and final stage is known as "revival" pruning. This type of pruning, for which a saw is used, will revive a tree that has become unproductive because of age or lack of care. Excess branches are cut back close to the trunk. A tree pruned by this method will not bear fruit for two years, but will return to normal production after about six years.

■ Refining

The technique of refining olive and other vegetable oils (sunflower, corn, etc.) developed during the late nineteenth century, and is thus relatively recent. The goal is to eliminate non-lipid substances from the oil, in order to obtain a product with a longer shelf life (see Storage) that is "purer," visually more translucent, and resistant to oxidation.

Refining is a chemical process that eliminates undesirable substances such as toxic mildew, fatty acids, trace metals, and insecticide residues. Cleansing destroys all traces of soap and soda, while wax removal skims off residues that do not dissolve at low temperatures. The oil is then bleached and deodorized, i.e. cleansed of all the volatile substances that give it its distinctive taste and aroma.

This chemical miracle thus eliminates the very qualities that are particularly sought after in olive oil: flavor (which makes it so popular for gastronomy*), pigments, and the vitamins and antioxidants beneficial to health*. In France*, the sale of pure refined olive oil is simply prohibited. In other countries—Turkey, for example—it is often used to "cut" virgin olive oil.

In Nyons (France), AOC (Origin Officially Guaranteed) oil is pressed from a single variety of olive, the *tanche*.

Regions

The olive tree's native regions reflect its history. Research shows that the olive originally came from Asia Minor, and subsequently spread throughout the Mediterranean Basin. It is now found primarily in countries that have continued the cultivation* of this ancient tree, despite the changes in diet and agriculture characteristic of the early twentieth century. In Western Europe, the two principal producing countries are still Spain* and Italy*. During the past century, France*, formerly a top producer, has fallen to seventh place among European growers, which rank as follows: Spain* (about five million acres); Italy* (2.5 million acres); Greece* (just under two million acres); Portugal* (about 750,000 acres); Albania, the former Yugoslavia, France, and Malta (only five hundred acres). Tunisia (see North Africa) is the main olive growing country on the African continent (over 3.5 million acres), followed by Morocco, Algeria, Libya, and Egypt. Countries that have only recently planted olive trees* include South Africa (2,500 acres), Angola, and Australia (five thousand acres).

In the Middle East* and Asia the leaders are Turkey* (two million acres) and Syria (just under one million acres), followed by Palestine, Lebanon, Israel, Cyprus, Jordan, Iraq, and Iran. China, a newcomer to the field, already boasts a production equal to that of France.

On the American continent, olives are primarily produced in the regions originally colonized by Spain* and Portugal*. These include Argentina (about 75,000 acres), Mexico, Chile, Peru, Uruguay, and Brazil. The United States has only about 30,000 acres of olive groves, 99 percent of them in California.

Olive grove, Lebanon.

■ Religion

The olive tree*, emblem of the Mediterranean, has influenced all of the religions that developed in the area. In Antiquity* olive oil fueled the lamps* that burned continuously in sacred temples, whether Egyptian or Hebrew, Greek or Roman. When consecrated, it was used to anoint both Judaic and Christian kings. This consecrated oil* is still used today for the Christian rites of baptism, confirmation, extreme unction, and the ordination of priests. Olive oil is mentioned frequently in the Bible (140 times), as is the olive tree (100 times), which is considered the king of all trees: "The trees ... said to the olive tree, Reign thou over us. But the olive tree said unto them, Should I leave my fatness wherewith by me they honour God and man, and go to be promoted over the trees?" (Judges 9:8–9).

In the story of the flood, a dove bearing an olive leaf in its beak signals the end of God's wrath to Noah: "And he stayed yet another seven days; and again he sent forth the dove out of the ark; And the dove came in to him in the evening; and, lo, in her mouth was an olive leaf pluckt off: so Noah knew that the waters were abated from the earth." (Genesis 8:10–11).

For Islam, the olive tree is a symbol* of the Prophet's presence: thanks to this blessed tree, humankind enjoys the light given out by the oil lamp, a divine light that brings men closer to Allah.

Noah Sending the Animals Away from the Ark (on the left, the dove bearing an olive branch to Noah). Mosaic, thirteenth century A.D. Saint Mark's Basilica, Venice.

Jean Leblanc's specialist oil shop, Paris.

Shop interior, Nice.

■ Shops

Compared with the number of shops specializing exclusively in wine, coffee, or tea, there exist only a few devoted entirely to olive oil. High quality oil was once sold only in specialist grocery stores, and today it can be found most easily at smart shops in big cities, such as Balducci's and Zabar's in New York, or Harrod's and Fortnum and Mason in London. Today, olive oil of acceptable (if not superb) quality is also sold in supermarkets.

The *Oliviers & Co* chain has revolutionized this sector with the creation of "tasting shops" presenting a broad selection of growths*, including the best varieties* from around the Mediterranean. These shops, which have branches in London and New York (including one in Grand Central Station), have revived the tradition of selection by name and origin. Customers first taste the oils, which are labeled by location and date of pressing, thus guaranteeing quality and freshness.

Note that many olive mills are open to visitors and also have on-site shops, and that most will fill orders by mail. See the addresses at the back of this book for further details.

Her mother filled a basket with all manner of food to the heart's desire, dainties too she set therein, and she poured wine into a goat-skin bottle, while Nausicaa climbed into the wain. And her mother gave her soft olive oil also in a golden cruse . . .

Homer, *The Odyssey*

Right: Antique oil pump, Oliviers & Co, Paris.

Savon de Marseille manufactured by Marius Fabre, Salon-de-Provence, near Marseilles.

■ Soap

Soap is apparently an invention of the ancient Gauls, who made it from a mixture of potash and tallow. This is borne out by the fact that the ancient Latin word for soap (*sapo*) comes from the Celtic language. Tallow was soon replaced by olive oil, which was boiled with water, mixed with ashes, and then filtered to obtain an emulsion. The Arabs perfected soap made with olive oil by adding lime to its composition.

"Modern" soap made its first appearance during the ninth century. A solid substance made with olive oil, it was

Marseilles was granted a monopoly and became dominant in the market. Local manufacture of this valuable product was placed under close supervision, and a quality label established: the famed *Savon de Marseille*. In the nineteenth century the use of soda became more common, olive oil was replaced by less costly oils (such as peanut), and Marseilles fell from popularity.

Savon de Marseille was traditionally made by heating olive oil paste with soda, rinsing the mixture to extract the soda, and spreading the residue in large sheets. The sheets were then cut into blocks weighing approximately 60 pounds each, and dried on screens made of cane. Lastly, the soap was molded into cubic cakes and embossed with the name of the manufacturer. The classic *Savon de Marseille* made with olive oil is indisputably the most natural, and one of the least costly, although the large cubic cakes are somewhat unwieldy. Unfortunately, many soaps sold in this form are totally unrelated to the original product made with olive oil, and very few soap manufacturers still follow the old recipe. Marius Fabre, the famous centuries-old brand, still produces "genuine" Marseilles soap, in Salon-de-Provence. An olive-cake content of at least 72 percent is specified for this green colored soap. With an annual production of 1,000 tons, Marius Fabre now exports to the United States and Japan. The traditional French washerwoman's soap has now become a fashionable ecological choice around the world.

first produced in Marseilles and the surrounding region. The use of soap spread during the Crusades, and the Italian cities of Savone (from which the French and Italian words for soap are derived), Venice*, and Genoa became major producers. In the seventeenth century, the soap industry in

Nuñez de Prado olive grove, Baena, Andalusia.

■ SPAIN

Twenty years ago, due to over-production, the European Economic Community was forced to subsidize the uprooting of olive trees. Today, by contrast, in response to increased demand, subsidies are awarded for planting.

Spain is the leading producer world-wide of olive oil, and the most indus-trialized. Its major labels, such as Anfora and Borges, produce oil which is sold throughout the world. Spanish olive groves cover a total of more than five million acres. The groves in Andalusia are particularly impressive: hundreds of acres of olive groves blanket the hillsides with their endless rows of rustling, silvery leaves.

In addition to this mass production market, the Spaniards have also developed a premium market covering six AOC (Origin Officially Guaranteed) areas that produce exceptional growths*. These are: Siurana and Los Garrigues, near Barcelona, in Catalonia; Baena, Priego de Cordoba, Sierra Magina, and Sierra Segura in Andalusia. For some of these growths, the maximum acidity level is fixed at 0.4 percent (Baena) or 0.5 perent (Los Garrigues, Sierra Magina, Siurana). Baena oil—sunshine yellow in color, without the slightest glint of green—is the most highly prized of all Spanish oils. Its mild, almost sweet flavor makes it especially suitable for use in dessert recipes.

Most Spanish olive groves are found in Andalusia: the countryside would be hard to imagine without its olive and orange trees, its vast plateaus dotted with sheep and bulls. Here, large cooperatives* are the rule, although some small independent mills* are still active. Large family-owned estates cultivate *fleur d'olive* oil, i.e. the premium oil drained from olives prior to pressing*. This connoisseur product envelopes the palate in aromas of ripe olive and citrus fruit, accented with a distinctive spicy note. The labels of the best producers, such as Nuñez de Prado, always include the region of origin and date of pressing. Andalusia is also the region of Spain most noted for its gastronomy*, and olive oil is omnipresent in its magnificent recipes.

Squid and Red Peppers in Baena Oil

In springtime, the Spanish countryside is carpeted with golden yellow broom, which once played a starring role in the kitchen. When steeped in olive oil, broom flowers (also used in perfumery) add a delicious accent. It is featured in this recipe for white squid and red peppers glowing with the colors of the Andalusian hacienda.

Serves 4
• 6 red bell peppers
• 1 pound small white squid
• 1 handful yellow broom blossoms (optional)
• fresh mint leaves
• 1 cup plus 4–5 tablespoons olive oil

Prepare the aromatic oil: Place ten fresh mint leaves cut into julienne strips in a cup of olive oil, season with salt and pepper, add the (optional) yellow broom flowers. Stir. Allow to marinate for 24 hours.
Grill the whole peppers until the skin can be removed easily. Peel, remove seeds, cut into strips, and marinate in 4–5 tablespoons olive oil seasoned with salt and pepper. Clean the squid and steam for three minutes (maximum). Strain the marinade and pour over the squid. Serve the peppers and squid with toast (rubbed with garlic and oil if desired) as an hors d'œuvre.
Accompany with an Andalusian Fino sherry, a fruity full-bodied white wine, or a chilled Muscat.

■ Storage

Although olive oil is less unstable than most other vegetable oils, appropriate precautions should nevertheless be taken for storing it. Like wine, olive oil must be stored away from air and light to prevent it from becoming rancid (i.e. oxidizing). Opaque containers are preferable and, once a bottle or can of oil has been opened, its contents should be consumed entirely before opening another one.

In countries where consumption is high, olive oil is often stored in large earthenware jars kept in a cellar. Bottles for table service are then regularly filled from the jars. Containers of olive oil should be kept tightly shut and never stored in an enclosed space where there are strong odors, such as the refrigerator. Oils with flavorings* (herbs or spices) will deteriorate more rapidly and should be consumed promptly. Although some oils contain chemical additives that retard deterioration, pure oils are always preferable.

For those who live near an olive mill*, the best solution is to purchase freshly pressed oil after the annual harvest. This oil can be stored for one to two years.

■ Symbolism

In Antiquity*, the Greeks associated olive trees* with the goddess Athena (see Mytho-logy), who personified wisdom and the military arts: she was a valiant warrior. The wreaths presented to wise men and the

Olive oil storeroom, Nuñez de Prado, Baena, Andalusia.

winners of athletic contests during that era were woven sometimes of laurel, and sometimes of olive branches. The Romans, for their part, attributed the olive branch to the goddess of peace. For Christianity and Judaism, the olive tree—ever green and generous with its fruit—is the symbol of abundance, eternal life, and peace: in the Old Testament, the dove bearing an olive leaf in its beak to Noah announces the end of the divine wrath, and the ebbing of the flood waters. Christians also associate the olive tree specifically with Jesus Christ. On Palm Sunday, the last Sunday in Lent, fresh branches of olive, laurel, or palm are carried in the procession commemorating Christ's solemn entry into Jerusalem.

The olive tree also symbolizes purity, immortality, and resurrection. Christ climbed the Mount of Olives to meditate and pray there; the cross of the crucifixion was made of cedar and olive woods. The cross represents a sort of cosmic tree, harbinger of a better world. For Muslims, the olive tree symbolizes the "axis of the world," a Tree of Paradise bringing mankind divine light (see Lamp), and "On each of its leaves is written one of the names of Allah." The olive tree was brought to southern Asia (probably from Persia) in the third millennium B.C. The symbolism connected with the olive tree in this part of the world is similar to that characteristic of the West. In India, the olive tree is a symbol of peace, used to calm the furies of both nature and humankind; in Japan it is a symbol of good intentions, a pledge of peace and success; in China, where its green fruits represent life and longevity, it was once used to make a beverage served at the New Year.

Elisabeth Vigée-Lebrun (1755–1842), *Peace accompanying Abundance.* Oil on canvas. Musée du Louvre, Paris.

■ TAPENADE
A Condiment Made
With Olives

The word "tapenade" is derived from *tupeno*, the Provençal term for caper. This condiment is made of crushed olives, capers, desalted anchovies, olive oil, lemon juice, and spices. The olives can be either green or black, and some recipes call for the addition of garlic, mustard, thyme, bay leaf, etc. In Italy* tapenade is served on bread rubbed with oil, and in Provence on toast or as a garnish for raw vegetables, grilled meat, and so on.

Tapenade reflects a very old tradition: olive pastes were sold by street vendors in ancient Athens; in Rome, raw olives or olive paste formed part of the *gustatio* (appetizer) served as the first course at mealtime. Columella recorded the recipe for *tapenade:* "In fine weather, pick very ripe black olives and spread them on reeds, in the shade, for an entire day. The next day ... place the crushed olives in a new basket which is then subjected to the action of the press in order to collect the oil. The paste is then placed on grinding stones that have been well cleansed: it is mixed by hand with salt that has been torrefied and pounded, and other dry seasonings such as fenugreek, cumin, fennel seed and Egyptian anis. Oil is then added, so that the paste will not dry out; this should be done, moreover, whenever the paste appears dry. But this wonderful taste will last no more than two months. For this condiment, it is preferable to use olives from Calabria, known as oleasters because they resemble the fruit of the wild olive tree*."

■ Taster

Oil tasters are comparable to wine tasters: following a chemical analysis verifying the soundness of the product, tasters evaluate quality by sipping small amounts. They must determine whether the oil will age properly during the two years it remains on the market; whether it is consistent with its reputation; and its value in terms of gastronomy*.

There are very few olive oil tasters. Wine taster Eric Verdier also works as an olive oil taster. "Unlike wine," he explains, "olive oil does not characteristics. As with wine, the vocabulary used evokes analogies: "notes" of artichoke, citrus fruit, flowers, green apple, etc. Tasting is carried out in three stages: an initial, visual evaluation, to make sure that the product is clear and transparent (except for the oils drained from unripe fruit, which remain cloudy but have a brief shelf life); this is followed by an olfactory evaluation of the aroma; then comes the tasting *per se*, on the palate, to confirm the aroma and to test for bitterness. Some tasters employ an old Corsican technique. When they visit olive mills*, they rub a few drops of oil into the palm of their hand. The hand's heat brings out the oil's aroma. This is an effective technique for identifying any possible problems such as rancidity, the odor of fermented straw, vinous or burnt notes and so on.

Eric Verdier has established a classification* ranking eight extra virgin olive oils in five categories: ordinary (mass market brands); selected (good blended oils,); second class (elegant oils, without smoky accents); first class (the equivalent of growths* for wine); and prime for the few very great oils. Tasters must also evaluate each oil for its value in relation to its retail cost*, and understand how it will be used in the kitchen, since oils are rarely consumed pure, but are usually associated with a range of spices and foodstuffs.

Francisco Nuñez de Prado, olive oil taster for Nuñez de Prado in Baena, Andalusia.

have a strong bouquet. It possesses only seventy-seven dominant molecules, compared with a thousand for pepper! Our work thus consists in identifying characteristics that may be extremely subtle, but are crucial to quality."

Tasters must first check the oil's content in oleic acids (the less there are, the more healthy the oil) and in the natural phenols that protect it against bacterial contamination. They then identify the oil's aromatic

Olive grove, Turkey.

■ TURKEY

Turkey is one of the oldest homes for the olive grove. Today, with over two million acres under cultivation, it ranks fourth worldwide. However, Turkish olive oil is not a common sight on supermarket shelves in Europe, since priority is given to products originating in the European Union, and Turkey has difficulty finding markets for its stock elsewhere. The area that is now Turkey, once dominated by the Greeks and later by the Romans, produced the best oils available in Antiquity*. When the Byzantine Empire fell to the Ottomans (with the conquest of Constantinople in 1453), the sultans established new mills*, improved quality, and awarded the olive a privileged place in their sophisticated gastronomy*.

Turkish production is still fragmented today with 320,000 independently owned groves, but processing is largely carried out by major national cooperatives* controlled by the government, such as the Taris Cooperative (15,000 members) and the Marmara Birlik Cooperative (30,000 members).

Izmir (formerly Smyrna), on the Aegean coast, is the Turkish capital of olive oil. Roadside mills* abound in the region. Farther north, around Bergama (formerly Pergamum), miles of olive groves sway in the breeze beneath the frequently snow-covered Kas mountains that provide natural irrigation* during the summer thaw. These groves are several centuries old. Nearby lies the city of Ayvalik, inhabited by Greeks until 1920, once a center for the production of olive oil and its derivatives such as soap*. Although no longer pre-eminent, it is still a major center for the industry. In this region, which produces the best Turkish oil, olive trees are cultivated using the same methods as centuries ago. At harvest time, men prod the olives off the trees with long poles, while their womenfolk gather them off the ground by hand, as they have done for hundreds of years.

Turkey is currently the major beneficiary of the recent fad for olive oil in the United States. The cost* of Turkish oil is lower than that for Western European oils and most importantly, Turkey produces a blend of virgin and refined oils known as "Riviera" that has a milder taste than pure virgin olive oil, and thus appeals to the American palate.

During the Ottoman era (1453–1922), the sultans' court at Istanbul was one of the most sophisticated centers for aristocratic cuisine. The Turkish gastronomic tradition is exceptional, and its influence still extends to the ancient empire's former territories in North Africa*, Greece*, and the Middle East*.

The people of Turkey have no peers when it comes to spices and olive oil. Roses, often combined with olive oil, are one of their favorite flavorings, particularly for desserts.

Sautéed Eggplant with Honey and Roses

The cuisine inherited from the Ottoman empire is among the most sophisticated in the world, and one of only two in the Mediterranean Basin (the other is Morocco) to feature sweet-sour dishes. Eggplant is particularly appreciated for its ability to absorb olive oil like a sponge, considerably enhancing the somewhat bland natural flavor of this vegetable.

Serves 4
• 4 firm, ripe eggplants
• 1 cup floral honey
• 1 tablespoon rosewater
• 1 rose blossom
(unsprayed, preferably *rosa damascena*)
• juice of 1 lemon
• olive oil

Cut the washed, unpeeled eggplants lengthwise into very thin slices. Dip the slices in olive oil and sauté in a skillet. When the eggplant slices are golden (almost burned), remove them from the skillet and drain on absorbent paper. Melt the honey (if it is not completely liquid) in a pot with the lemon juice. Do not allow to boil. When the liquid mixture is hot, add the rosewater and a few rose petals. Pour over the eggplant. Decorate with the remaining rose petals. Serve lukewarm.

Accompany with a full-bodied red wine like a Zinfandel or even a great Bordeaux, for example a Château Haut-Brion.

■ VARIETIES
Over Five Hundred Species

There are over five hundred species of olive. Some olive trees* are grown mainly for yield, others for their ornamental value. Different species are cultivated for the production of olives and olive oil, respectively. The major oil-producing varieties include: in Greece*, *koroneiki* and *mastoidis*; in Italy*, *caratina, frantoio, leccino, moraiolo*; in Spain*, *arbequina, cornicabra, empeltre, hojiblanca, lechin, picual*; and in France*, *aglandau, picholine*, and *tanche*. Specific varieties are selected according to the local climate and the harvesting* schedule: harvesting in an olive grove planted with different varieties maturing at different times can begin in late summer and continue through mid-winter.

In general, green olives—highly appreciated whether bottled or canned—are not used for oil. This is because green olives, which are unripe by definition, yield oil with an underdeveloped bouquet, and in smaller volumes. On the other hand, green olive oil is considered by some connoisseurs to be the purest of all, and the people of Antiquity* prized it for its considerable cosmetic* virtues.

The selection criteria for olive trees reflect extremely ancient customs: with the exception of newly established groves (in China, for example), most olive groves are planted primarily with native varieties that have remained unchanged over the centuries. In the Languedoc region of France, growers are once again producing the *lucques* variety. These olives are delicious in cooking and on the table, and also yield an interesting oil.

Most oils on the market are balanced blends of several varieties, but there is a new interest in oils made from a single variety, in imitation of the "growth*" principle for wines. Blends contain an empirical combination of the varieties produced by a single estate, village, or region. The mill* will either combine the different varieties prior to crushing* and pressing*, or blend the different oils before bottling. In any case, because olive trees yield fruit only once every two years and volume is extremely variable, a more standardized method would meet with only irregular success. This also explains why oils marketed by small independent producers often show differences in quality from one year to the next. Some large producers, such as Borges in Spain and the major French cooperatives (Nyons, Clermont-l'Hérault) are able to benefit from volume, marketing blends that are more consistent, or oils pressed from a single variety, which will then be mentioned on the label: *frantoio, hojiblanca, lucques, picholine*, etc. This is a recent trend, however, and not favoured by all producers.

Far left: *cayet roux*
Left: *salonenque*

Far left: *tanche*
Left: *lucques*

Far left: *cailletier*
Left: *picholine*

Far left: *cayon*
Left: *bouteillan*

■ Venice

It was during the First Crusade (1096–99) that Venice began to establish trading posts in the Orient. In exchange for financial and military support, Venice was awarded trading privileges throughout the Byzantine empire. After the Fourth Crusade (1202–04), which Venice had diverted into an attack on Constantinople in order to pillage its wealth, the Most Serene Republic expropri-ated extensive territories: Euboea, Morea, and Crete, one of the foremost producers of olive oil. Venice then extended its influence to Corfu (in 1386), the coasts of Albania and Dal-matia—re-conquered between 1409 and 1420—and Cyprus (in 1489). At that point, Venice dominated trade, and particu-larly the olive oil trade, through-out the Mediterranean.

Throughout this economic area, the maritime republic's goal was

not just to control traditional trade, but also to meet the growing demand for olive oil in soap* manufacturing and textile processing (wool oiling). At harvest time, the Venetians purchased olives off the tree in southern Italy*, processed them, and marketed the oil (at considerable profit) throughout Europe.

They also established olive groves on their conquered territories of Crete and Corfu, organizing trade in the oil on a vast scale.

In 1497, when the Portuguese explorer Vasco da Gama opened a route to the Indies, the Portuguese merchant navy threatened Venice's monopoly of the spice trade. It was at this time that Venice began its gradual decline, losing forever its virtual monopoly of the olive oil trade. On the European and American markets, Italian and Greek oils soon gave way to those marketed by Portugal.

Canaletto, *Riva degli Schiavoni, circa* 1736. Oil on canvas. Sir John Soane's Museum, London.

Museums and Institutions

International Olive Oil Council
Principe de Vergara, 154
28002 Madrid
Spain
Tel.: 91 5903638
The IOOC is a UN-chartered body that regulates olive oil throughout most of the world, but not the United States.

California Olive Oil Council
P.O. Box 7520
Berkeley, CA 94707-0520
USA
Tel.: (888) 718-9830
The Certification body for Californian olive oil, which represents 99 percent of American produce.

Olive Institute
40, place de la Libération
26110 Nyons
France
Tel.: 04 75 26 90 90
An information center opened in 1996 in France's "olive capital."

Nyons Olive Museum
Place Olivier-de-Serres
26110 Nyons
France
Tel.: 04 75 26 12 12
Museum dedicated to the industry that made the fortune of this town.

Mills and producers

France

AOC Nyons
Moulin Autrand-Dozol
Le Pont Roman
26110 Nyons
Tel.: 04 75 26 02 52

AOC Les Baux
Château d'Estoublon
13990 Fontvieille
Tel.: 04 90 54 64 00

Moulin Jean-Marie Cornille
Coopérative de la vallée des Baux
13520 Maussane
Tel.: 04 90 54 32 37

Christian Rossi
Quartier Saint-Éloi
13831 Châteaurenard
Tel.: 04 90 94 02 00

Val Doré
Coopérative La Cravenco
Route d'Eyguières
13280 Raphèle-les-Arles
Tel.: 04 90 54 75 37

Provence
Moulin La Balméenne
Avenue Jules-Ferry
84190 Beaumes-de-Venise
Tel.: 04 90 62 94 15

Haute-Provence
Moulin des Pénitents
04190 Les Mées
Tel.: 04 92 34 07 67

Nice region
Roger Michel
Moulin de la Bragues
06650 Opio–Le Rouret
Tel.: 04 93 77 23 03

Languedoc
Coopérative
de Clermont-l'Hérault
13, av. du Président-Wilson
34800 Clermont-l'Hérault
Tel.: 04 67 96 10 36

Italy

Tuscany
Castello Banfi
53024 Montalcino
Tel.: 057 7840111

Castello di Cacchiano
Gaiole
53010 Monti in Chianti
Tel.: 057 7747267

Castello di Volpaia
53017 Radda in Chianti
Tel.: 057 7738066

Fattoria dei Barbi
53024 Montalcino
Tel.: 057 7848277

Fattoria Maionchi
Toffori
55012 San Gennaro
Tel.: 058 3978194

Frantoio de Santa Tea
50066 Santa Tea, Florence
Tel.: 055 868117

Poggio Antico
53024 Montalcino
Tel.: 057 7848044

Tenuta La Chiesa
57037 Portoferraio
Tel.: 056 5933046

Tenuta di Forci
Via per Pieve Santo Stefano, 7165
55060 Lucca
Tel.: 058 3349001

Sicily
Barbera & figli
Via E. Amari, 55a
90139 Palermo
Tel.: 091 582900

Ravidà
Via Roma, 173
92013 Menfi
Tel.: 092 571109

Apulia
Caroli Stefano
C. da Trazzonara, 526
74015 Martina Franca
Tel.: 080 700402

Clemente
Vico dei Francescani, 3
71043 Manfredonia
Tel.: 088 4582033

Cuonzo Franco M.
Corso Vittore Emanuele, 22
70036 Palombaio di Bitonto
Tel.: 080 608012

Frantioi Elli Galantino
Via Corato, 2

70052 Bisceglie
Tel.: 080 3921320

Pellegrino
La Spineta
70031 Andria
Tel.: 088 3569763

Calabria
Donnavascia
Azienda agricola Acconia
88022 Acconia di Curinga
Tel.: 096 878057

Liguria
Tenuta dell' Ornellaia
57020 Bolgheri
Tel.: 056 5762140

Spain

Catalonia
Aceites Borges
Av. José Trepat
25300 Tàrrega
Tel.: 97 3501212

Oleastrum-Olis de Catalunya
Av. Sant Jordi, 17–19
43021 Reus
Tel.: 97 7340387

Andalusia
Oleo Mágina
Carretera de Úbeda
–Iznalloz km 86
23568 Bélmez de la
Moradela
Tel.: 95 3394012

Anfora-Columela
Av. del Aeropuerto, 3
14004 Cordoba
Tel.: 95 7761053

United States

Aeolia Organics LLC
P.O. Box 942
San Juan CA 95960
Tel.: (530) 292-3619
Fax: (530) 292-3688

Airola Olive Oil
2700 6th Ave.

Sacramento, CA 95818
Email: dairola@jps.net

B.R. Cohn/American
Classics
14301 Arnold Dr.
Glen Ellen, CA 95442
Tel.: (707) 938-4460
Fax: (707) 939-3679

Big Paw Grub
P.O. Box 863
Calistoga, CA 94515-0863
Tel.: (707) 967-9718

Burgard & Siday Olive Co.
6850 Hwy. 41E
Templeton, CA 93465
Tel.: (805) 466-5566
Fax: (805) 462-9527
Email: csidah@tcsn.net
www.growolives.com

Calaveras Olive Oil
Company Inc.
655 O'Byrnes Ferry Rd.
P.O. Box 344
Copperopolis, CA 95228
Tel.: (209) 785-1000
Fax: (209) 785-1100

Frantoio Olive Oil Co.
152 Shoreline Hwy.
Mill Valley, CA 94941
Tel.: (415) 289-5777
Fax: (415) 289-5775
www.frantoio.com

Gold Hill Retreat
& Olive Co.
P.O. Box 744
Lotus, CA 95651
Tel.: (530) 621-7073

Henwood Estate Olive Oil
6735 Hammonton
Smartwood Rd.
Marysville, CA 95091
Tel.: (530) 639-2400

Villa Gigli
145 Hot Springs Road
P.O. Box 307
Markleeville, CA 96021
Tel.: (530) 694-2253
Fax: (530) 694-2253

Willow Creek Olive Ranch
8530 Vineyard Dr.
Paso Robles, CA 93446
Tel.: (805) 239-7632

Olive Oil Shops and Products

Barclay Crocker Soaps
47, Job's Lane
Southampton, NY 11968
USA
Tel.: (631) 283-8012

French Soaps Ltd.
P.O. Box 3639
Newport, RI 02840
USA
Tel.: (888) 511-7900
www.frenchsoaps.com

Olive Merchant & Co.
P.O. Box 2559
Aptos, CA 95001
USA
Tel.: (877) 986-5483

Oliviers & Co. Inc.
10, E 39th St, 8th Floor
New York, NY 10016
USA
Tel.: (212) 696-9438

Oliviers & Co. London
114, Ebury St.
London SW1 2QR
England
Tel.: 0207 823 6770

The Oil and Spice Shop
The Butlers Wharf Building
36e, Shad Thames
London SE1 2YE
England
Tel.: 0207 403 4030

The Oil Merchant
47 Ashchurch Grove
London W12 9BU
England
Tel.: 0208 740 1335

INDEX

SELECTED BIBLIOGRAPHY

Chibois, Jacques, and Olivier Baussan. *Olive Oil.* Paris: Flammarion, 2000.

Dolamore, Anne. *The Essential Olive Oil Companion.* Northampton, MA: Interlink, 1999.

Gordon-Smith, Clare. *Basic Flavorings: Olive Oil.* Philadelphia: Courage Books, 1996.

Harwood, John. *A Handbook of Olive Oil: Analysis and Properties.* Gaithersburg, MD: Aspen, 1999.

Irvine, Sian. *Olive Oil: Fresh Recipes from Leading Chefs.* Boston, MA: Charles E. Tuttle Co., 2000.

Knickerbocker, Peggy. *Olive Oil: From Tree to Table.* San Francisco: Chronicle Books, 1997.

Midgley, John. *The Goodness of Olive Oil.* New York: Random House, 1992.

Pellechia, Thomas. *Garlic, Wine and Olive Oil: Historical Anecdotes and Recipes.* Santa Barbara: Capra, 2000.

Rogers, Ford. *Olives: Cooking with Olives and their Oils.* Berkeley, CA: Ten Speed Press, 1995.

Taylor, Judith. *The Olive in California: History of an Immigrant Tree.* Berkeley, CA: Ten Speed Press, 2000.

Photographic credits: BERLIN, Bildarchiv Preussischer Kulturbesitz 39; LONDON, Sir John Soane's Museum 114–115; Jean-Loup Charmet 20, 67, 78, 79, 98; Dagli Orti 8, 9, 22, 26, 88, 94–95, 97; Diaf/J.-C. Gérard 93; P. Duvochel 56; F.-X. Emery 13 bottom, 15; Flammarion archives 47 top, 71, 76 left, 80; Pierre Ginet 107; A. Gualina 113; Hoa Qui/Philippe Roy 60/E. Valentin 110; Jacana/Sylvain Cordier 72–73; Magnum/Bruno Barbey 63/Erich Lessing 74–75 top, 90–91; J. Marando 30–31; PARIS, Musées/Karin Maucotel 66 top; Réunion des musées nationaux 38, 76–77, 102–103; Scope/J. Guillard 13 top, 24 bottom, 27, 34–35, 40 bottom, 48–49 top, 58, 68–69, 86–87 top, 89, 108/Michel Gotin 99/Jean-Luc Barde 104–105; Sunset/J.-M. Fichaux 12, 42, 43/B. Letnap 36; Tréal/J.-M. Truiz 11; Jean-Charles Vaillant 6, 16, 17 top, 17 bottom, 19, 25, 29, 33 bottom, 35, 40 top, 41, 54–55, 64, 83, 109; SALON-DE-PROVENCE, Crea photo/Jean-François Lepage 100–101; TOULOUSE, Musée des Augustins 70; VANVES, Explorer/Francis Jalain 10; Nicolas de Barry 21, 24 top, 33 top, 46, 49 bottom, 50–51, 52–53, 57, 59, 65, 69 bottom, 75 bottom, 85 bottom, 87 bottom, 111.

All quotations from Homer's *Odyssey* are taken from the A. Lang and S. Butcher translation, published by Harvard Classics, New York: P.F. Collier and Son, 1909.

Translated and adapted from the French by Louise Guiney
Copy-editing: Caroline Mackenzie, Context, Marseilles
Typesetting: Claude-Olivier Four
Color separation: Pollina S.A., France

Originally published as *L'ABCdaire de l'huile d'olive* © 1999 Flammarion
English-language edition © 2001 Flammarion
All rights reserved. No part of this publication may be reproduced in any form or by any means
without written permission from the publishers.

ISBN: 2-08010-586-8
N° d'édition: FA0586-01-VII
Dépôt légal: 10/2001
Printed and bound by Pollina S.A., France - n° L84364